AF470215

Nottinghamshire

Charles Wildgoose

COUNTRYSIDE BOOKS
NEWBURY BERKSHIRE

First published 2010
© Charles Wildgoose 2010

All rights reserved. No reproduction
permitted without the prior permission
of the publisher:

COUNTRYSIDE BOOKS
3 Catherine Road
Newbury, Berkshire

To view our complete range of books,
please visit us at
www.countrysidebooks.co.uk

ISBN 978 1 84674 184 5

Designed by Peter Davies, Nautilus Design
Produced through MRM Associates Ltd., Reading
Printed in Thailand

Contents

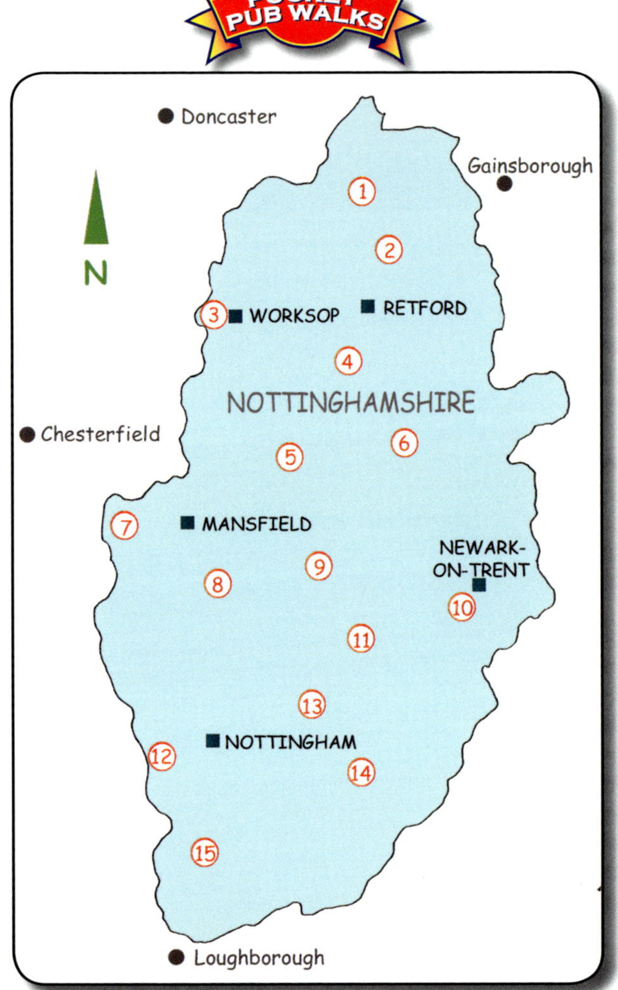

Area map showing location of the walks

Introduction

Living on the edge of the Peak District, as I do, it is all too easy to turn right at the bottom of the road and drive into the Dark or White Peaks to do a spot of walking. However, just lately, I've been turning left and driving to Nottinghamshire ... and, oh boy, have I enjoyed it.

There is some fine walking in Nottinghamshire. Sherwood Forest, the River Trent, Chesterfield Canal, Nottingham Canal, Grantham Canal, the Teversal Trail, the Southwell Trail and a medieval open field system – all feature within the pages of this book.

The idea is that you park at or near one of the pubs and set off for a morning's walk before getting back to the pub to enjoy a meal and a pint of beer ... or perhaps you prefer wine. English pubs need our patronage at this time so please support them.

Make sure you give yourself plenty of time too. I reckon to walk about two miles an hour but you may want to allow yourself a little more time, especially if you want to savour the delights of the countryside.

I would always recommend that you wear boots just in case the paths get a little muddy. There are some cross field paths here and there and so I wouldn't advise you wearing trainers, just in case. Take the relevant Ordnance Survey map too. Features can change and disappear and you will always feel more confident if you have a map to hand.

The walks have all been re-checked thoroughly and here I must say a big, big 'thank you' to Ruth, Graham and Tom Rhodes, together with their dog Mattie. They have been out in all weathers trekking along these routes and, in the process, thoroughly enjoying themselves (or so they tell me!).

A special and loving 'thank you' to ... well, she knows who she is ... for being there once again.

If there is one thing that sums up England to me, it's sitting in a village pub, a view of the church through the window, rooks calling out as they build their nests in the trees, a pint of beer on the table and a roaring log fire nearby ... oh, and a slice of steak and ale pie steaming on a plate in front of me. *That* is England to me. Hopefully you will get a flavour of this beautiful country we live in when you follow these walks through Nottinghamshire. Enjoy your walks.

Publisher's Note

We hope that you obtain considerable enjoyment from this book; great care has been taken in its preparation. However, changes of landlord and actual closures are sadly not uncommon. Likewise, although at the time of publication all routes followed public rights of way or permitted paths, diversion orders can be made and permissions withdrawn.

We cannot, of course, be held responsible for such diversion orders and any inaccuracies in the text which result from these or any other changes to the routes, nor any damage which might result from walkers trespassing on private property. We are anxious though that all details covering the walks and the pubs are kept up to date and would therefore welcome information from readers which would be relevant to future editions.

The simple sketch maps that accompany the walks in the book are based on notes made by the author whilst checking out the routes on the ground. For the benefit of a proper map, however, we do recommend that you purchase the relevant Ordnance Survey sheet covering your walk. The Ordnance Survey maps are widely available, especially through booksellers and local newsagents.

1 Everton

The Blacksmiths Arms

This fine walk allows you to escape from the crowds – the paths are good and the scenery interesting. The Barrow Hills Site of Special Scientific Interest is an especially exciting part of the route – there's even a seat in a lovely grassy glade where you can stop and take a breather. On the way round you walk past an old windmill beside the road that runs south from Everton to Mattersey. It was built in the mid 19th century and it's good to see that it hasn't fallen into disrepair. It is actually lived in.

Distance – 5¾ miles

OS Explorer 279 Doncaster GR 690912

A varied walk with much of interest – the section through the wood at Barrow Hills is particularly attractive.

Starting point The car park at the Blacksmiths Arms.

How to get there *Everton is on the A631, 3 miles east of Bawtry. Turn north into Chapel Lane in Everton. The pub car park is on the right immediately before Ferry Lane.*

THE PUB

The **Blacksmiths Arms** is one of those traditional pubs that we must not lose. It is full of character and low beams – one very low beam in particular. There are usually five cask ales available at any one time. At present the regular beers are Greene King IPA, John Smith's Cask and Old Peculier (the beer I would drink every day if I didn't have to watch my weight). Then there are a couple of guests such as Batemans XB and Black Sheep. Home-cooked food is served daily and you could expect to try Grimsby cod, steak and ale pie, or tuna and pasta bake from the menu. On the specials board there are dishes such as chicken, leek and ham pie or beef and Guinness. Various light bites and sandwiches are available too. The pub was established in 1749. As I say, it's a smashing pub.

Opening times are Monday 5.30 pm to 12 midnight; Tuesday to Friday 12 noon until 3 pm and 5.30 pm until 12 midnight; Saturday 12 noon until 2.30 pm and 4 pm until midnight. Food is available Tuesday to Saturday from 12 noon until 2.30 pm and from 6 pm until 9 pm; and on Sunday from 12 noon until 4 pm. ☎ *01777 817281*

1 Leave the pub car park by its entrance. Keep right to walk along **Ferry Lane** to reach the front of the pub. Bear left to reach the

church. Pass this on your left. Turn left at Everton village hall. Keep straight ahead into **Everton Sluice Lane**. About 70 yards after the last house on the left, turn left along the 'Restricted Byway'. Stay on this as it passes between high hawthorn hedges which are full of rabbit holes.

2 At a tarmac lane turn right past **Rock Cottage**, then left along **Pasture Lane**. After 600 yards, ignore the driveway swinging right towards **Pasture Farm**. Keep forward along the grassy green lane. Stay on this for nearly a mile as it gets narrower and narrower. Gradually the byway swings slowly left.

3 Where the hedges end in an open area (with a property 450 yards away to your right), turn left walking beyond the oak tree

Walking through the woodland on the Barrow Hills

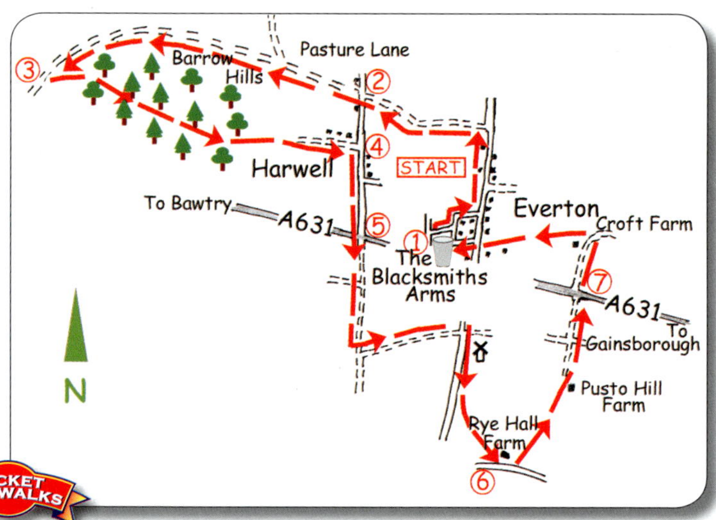

and, keeping a hedge on your left, enter the wood 150 yards later. In the wood follow the path directly uphill. Keep forward looking out for the odd yellow daub of paint signifying the path. At a crossroads of paths, keep forward. This is a delightful wood. Some way through the wood ignore a path joining the one you are on from the left. Pass a grassy clearing to your right. Just beyond this, the path forks. Take the right-hand fork, down a sandy path to reach a bridlegate. Here there's a panel for **Barrow Hills Sand Pit** SSSI, a nationally important reserve for flora and fauna including viper's bugloss. Just beyond the gate walk down the gravel track ahead. Keep forward for 200 yards.

4 Turn right along the lane in the village of **Harwell**. Stay on this to reach the A631.

5 Cross this, following the track on the other side for ½ mile. Turn left along another track. A third of a mile later, turn right alongside the road. Look out for **Mattersey Windmill** on your

left – how can you miss it? With **Sandy Garth** on your left, walk another 30 yards crossing a stile beyond a double gate. Enter the woodland beside a fence on your left and follow the path to a lane.

6 At the lane turn left past **Rye Hall Farm**. Enter **Pusto Hill Wood**, on your left, just beyond the farm. Where the bridleway splits, keep forward ignoring all paths to the right. The bridleway progresses through the wood to bring you to **Pusto Hill Farm**. Keep to the left of this and proceed along a grassy track. At a crossroads of tracks, keep forward to reach the A631.

7 Bear slightly left to follow the bridleway opposite leading to **Croft Farm**. After 350 yards, as the bridleway turns right, turn left along the driveway. Pass to the right-hand side of the bungalow (**Croft Farm**). Continue towards **Everton** in the distance. Some 300 yards beyond the bungalow, in the right-hand corner, pass through a gap into the field beyond and cross this to the field corner jutting out into a field 40 yards away. Walk along the left side of the field beyond to reach some houses. Cross a couple of stiles and keep forward into the houses. You reach a tarmac path with bungalows on your right. Keep forward to cross the road and walk along **Brewery Lane**, before bearing right into **Old Post Office Street**. Turn left along **Ferry Lane** to get back to the **Blacksmiths Arms**.

Places of interest nearby

Bassetlaw Museum in Retford is just 8 miles south of Everton and contains collections relating to local history, agriculture and archaeology. ☎ 01777 713749. **St Peter's church, Clayworth** has impressive murals on its interior walls. 01777 817688. Three miles to the south of Everton is the **Wetlands Animal Park** ☎ 01777 818099

2 Hayton

The Boat Inn

The thing that struck me about this walk was the amount of wildlife I saw, especially the pair of deer scurrying away across the far side of a field as I climbed to the highest part of the walk. I'm told there aren't many deer to be seen hereabouts. The walk runs along a Roman road at Haughgate Hill. As you walk down this old road bear in mind that it has been used for 2,000 years or more. You then swing northward up Northfield Leys Road – it is in fact nothing more than a track but its name implies that it too has a long and no doubt interesting history. Finally what about the last couple of miles of the walk alongside the Chesterfield Canal? Brilliant relaxing walking beside a lovely canal where, with luck, you'll see a narrowboat or two.

Distance – 6½ miles

OS Explorer 271 Newark-on-Trent GR 728851

You can get away from everyone on this walk. When I walked it on a sunny Sunday in September, I didn't see any other walkers.

Starting point The car park of the Boat Inn, or the small lay-by just over the canal bridge.

How to get there *Hayton is on the B1403 north of Clarborough (which is on the A620) to the north-east of Retford.*

THE PUB

The **Boat Inn** is in a lovely spot at the end of the village of Hayton beside the Chesterfield Canal. On a warm sunny day you can sit beside the canal and watch the narrowboats passing by. There are various beers on sale such as John Smith's, Stones Bitter, Davenports Highland Whisky Ale and Greene King IPA. The food is a revelation with specials such as carpaccio of octopus and lamb shank. The regular menu includes chunky Greek salad and penne vegetale (both vegetarian) as well as Cajun salmon. Steaks are on offer too and the fillet steak sizzler with oyster and marsala sauce and rice sounds very tempting. There's also a light bite menu from Monday to Saturday from 12 noon until 2 pm. Then there are baguettes and jacket potatoes and a fresh salad menu. On Sunday there is a carvery that is really good value.

Food is available during the week from 12 noon until 2 pm and from 5 pm until 9 pm; Saturday from 12 noon until 9 pm; and on Sunday from 12 noon until 4 pm. ☎ *01777 700158*

1 With your back to the front of the **Boat Inn**, turn left. Don't cross the canal bridge. Walk forward along **Burntleys Road**.

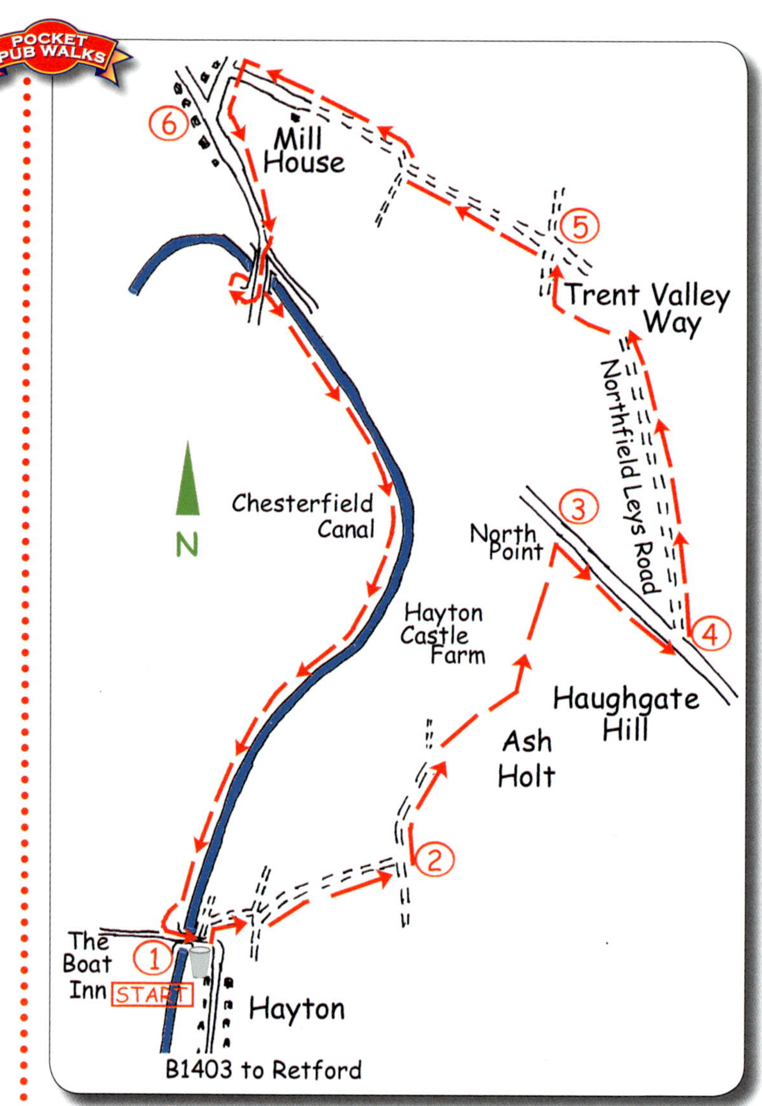
POCKET PUB WALKS
6
Mill House
5
Trent Valley Way
Northfield Leys Road
Chesterfield Canal
N
3
North Point
4
Hayton Castle Farm
Haughgate Hill
Ash Holt
2
The Boat Inn
1
START
Hayton
B1403 to Retford

In 20 yards swing right up the tarmac lane passing **Townend House**. At the top of the rise, turn right then almost immediately left along the stony byway. This rises steadily with far reaching views, especially behind you.

2 After half a mile, ignore the bridleway downhill to your right – bear left along the bridleway rising uphill to the left. Proceed towards a wood with good views on your left and West Burton power station on your right. Walk down the right side of the wood for 50 yards or so but then bear slightly right alongside a hedge on your left, ignoring a track running alongside the wood. Subsequently ignore a track forking left through a gate part way along the side of the field. Turn left after 150 yards, then immediately right, into a wood called **Ash Holt**. Proceed through the trees keeping in the same general direction as before. Leave the wood, walking along a hedgerow on your right. Half left is **Hayton Castle Farm**. Some 250 yards beyond the wood you reach another wood with the farm to your left. Pass through the gap on your right and walk alongside the trees on your left. Stay beside the wood to enter another field. Stay at the bottom side of this field, keeping forward at the end past a property called **North Point**.

3 Turn right uphill on the road. Climb the steep hill before the road levels out to then descend **Haughgate Hill**. This stretch is a Roman road. There are a couple of power stations in view now – West Burton on the left and Cottam on the right.

4 After ½ mile turn left up a track between hedges. This is **Northfield Leys Road**. Stay on this for two-thirds of a mile and note the electricity lines overhead. After walking under the second set (you will need to look out for them if the trees are in leaf) walk to the end of the first open field beyond the second set of electricity lines and turn left *inside* the field. (There may be a Trent Valley Way marker at this point.) Walk beside the hedge on your right, part of the **Trent Valley Way** though you may not

know it. At the end of the field, turn right along a green lane. By the time I'd got here when walking this route for the first time I'd seen a tiny toad, some partridges and a pair of deer.

5 On reaching a track turn left, rising gently to begin with. Where the track forks, ignore the track to the left (to Field Farm) by swinging right then left. Eventually, pass **Mill House** on your left. After this the standard of the route is racked up a bit – you're walking on tarmac! Turn left at the end of **Mill Lane** (the track you've been following).

6 Turn left at the main road in **Clayworth**. Ignore the road forking left to **North Wheatley** and on reaching and crossing the **Chesterfield Canal** turn right, then right again to pass under the bridge to the canal. Walk by the moorings of the **Retford and Worksop Boat Club**. For the rest of the walk, stay beside the canal. On reaching bridge 66 (a couple of miles later) rise up to the road before crossing it back to the **Boat Inn**.

Places of interest nearby

The **Wetlands Animal Park** is 3 miles to the south of Everton. ☎ 01777 818099. If you like looking around the inside of churches then **St Peter's church** in Clayworth might appeal to you. Look out in particular for the murals on its interior walls. ☎ 01777 817688. Or there's **St Mary's church** in Stow in Lincolnshire, some 10 miles east of Hayton which has been described as 'one of the most complete Saxon churches surviving in the country'. ☎ 01427 788251

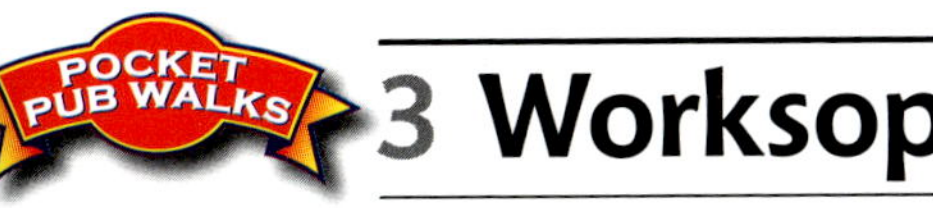

3 Worksop

The Lock Keeper

I'm a great fan of canals. It may have something to do with the fact that I am (very) distantly related to James Brindley, the man who was involved in the building of many English canals. He died in 1772, just a year or so into the building of the Chesterfield Canal but, even so, I like to think that I've been walking in his footsteps. In addition to the canal, there is the 17th-century Shireoaks Hall and the ponds in that vicinity. All in all, this walk may surprise you.

Distance – 5¼ miles

OS Explorers 270 Sherwood Forest and 279 Doncaster GR 572797

A level walk with a section beside the canal that you would be hard pressed to beat anywhere in England. You can have a cup of tea halfway round at Turnerwood Cottages.

Starting point The car park of the Lock Keeper but please park at the end furthest from the pub.

How to get there *Assuming you enter Worksop from Chesterfield to the west, on reaching the roundabout on the A57, take the second left following the A57 for Sheffield and Rotherham. At the next roundabout turn right for Tickhill before turning left almost immediately on the mini-roundabout to reach the Lock Keeper.*

THE PUB

The **Lock Keeper** is a Marstons' pub and, as such, Marstons' beers feature heavily, namely Pedigree and Smooth, as well as Banks's Bitter. The wide choice of food includes salmon, gammon steak, sirloin steak and Cajun chicken. There is also a carvery with three roasts on offer such as lamb, beef or turkey. If you fancy something lighter, then why not try one of the Lock Keeper's lite bites such as stuffed pepper or scampi. Sandwiches are also on offer if you want something lighter still.

Opening times are all day from noon until 11 pm.

☎ *01909 532565.*

1 From the pub, walk to the canal. Turn left. Pass under bridge 41. With the canal on your right continue to bridge 40 (built in 1999). Cross onto the other side of the canal and pass under the A57 (bridge 39b).

2 At **Doefield Dun Lock**, cross the lock and a metal footbridge across the overflow. Proceed with the canal on your right. On entering a field, keep the canal embankment on your right. At a pair of wooden electricity poles, the path (though keeping in the same direction) passes from the right side of the field to the left. There should be a stream on your left. At the end of the field cross a stile. Pass a house on your right, then a clubhouse. Follow the tarmac access to the end of the field. Where it swings right, turn left over a stone bridge. Keep forward along the obvious footpath with a hedge on your right, resisting the temptation to turn right into another field on crossing the bridge.

3 When you reach a lane, cross carefully. Walk along the stony track opposite. Pass whitewashed **Hall Cottage** on your right. This brings you to **Shireoaks Hall**. Pass through a gap beside a

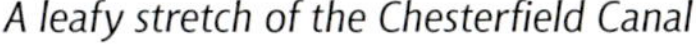

A leafy stretch of the Chesterfield Canal

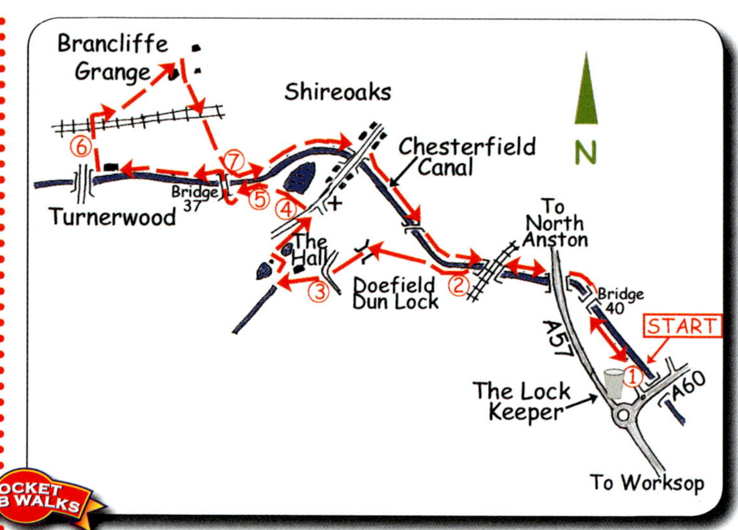

gate ahead, keeping the ha-ha on your right. At the end of the ha-ha, climb a stile before bearing right towards a pond ahead. Pass a long thin pond on your left as you go. On reaching the pond turn right, then left between the pond you were aiming for and a third pond. Pass a rather grand property to follow the track towards the village of Shireoaks. Bear right at the road into **Shireoaks**.

4 Before reaching the church, turn left immediately beyond **Shireoaks Village Garden**. This leads past **Bethel House** on your left. Pass the entrance to the cricket ground on your right. You should then see glimpses of a lake on your right. On reaching the gates of the Ranmoor Piscatorial Society, keep along the path beyond, to reach the canal again.

5 Turn left, keeping the canal on your right. Cross bridge 37 and turn left. Walk with the canal on your left. The Chesterfield Canal was started in 1771 and completed in 1777. The stone to rebuild

the Houses of Parliament in the 1830s passed along this canal. You reach the hamlet of **Turnerwood**. Turn right immediately beyond the last house on the right to descend into the garden beyond. You may get a cup of tea or coffee, or some locally-made ice cream at the little brick kiosk by the house (I can recommend this). In the garden, look out for the canal feeder on your right and walk beside it to the railway line.

6 Cross the line very carefully and turn right. Follow the feeder again to reach a track rising up into the wood on your left. Turn right though. Cross a stile by a long stone barn, turning left a few yards later with **Brancliffe Grange** ahead. After 70 yards, turn right at the bridleway at the end of the garden wall. Walk across the field and cross the railway line. Don't forget, 'STOP LOOK LISTEN'. Cross a stile into the field beyond. Bear slightly left into the second field. Then rise up to the canal to reach bridge 37 (rebuilt in 1996).

7 Turn left to **Shireoaks**. Cross the main road and continue with the canal still on your right. Pass the marina at bridge 38A. Continue along the canal all the way back to the start, remembering to cross to the other side at bridge 40.

Places of interest nearby

Creswell Crags is the only site in the UK where Ice Age paintings have been found. There's a short walk around the pond there and a new visitor centre. ☎ 01909 720378. **Bolsover Castle** sits on the edge of the village of Bolsover overlooking the lower ground away to the west. It is most impressive. ☎ 01246 822844. In Worksop itself there is of course the National Trust's **Mr Straw's House** where the contents of the house remain exactly as they were over 60 years ago. ☎ 01909 482380

4 Elkesley

The Robin Hood Inn

The first thing I noticed about Elkesley was the fact that, at present, the only way to and from it is via the A1 dual carriageway. The second thing I noticed is what an attractive churchyard it has. It's just a pity I couldn't get inside the church to look round. Halfway through the walk you enter the smaller, quieter village of Bothamsall. With its redbrick houses it really is quite delightful. Towards the end of the walk prepare to be delighted again by Elkesley Wood as you wind your way through it to reach a footbridge over the River Poulter. Wait a while on the bridge and try to spot the fish which will invariably show up. I'm sure I saw a pike the day I was there.

Distance – 5 miles

OS Explorer 270 Sherwood Forest GR 689755

A walk without any hills to speak of. Some of the paths may cross ploughed fields so make sure you wear your wellies or boots if the weather has been bad. It will be worth it though.

Starting point The car park of the Robin Hood Inn, or on the road by the church.

How to get there *Elkesley is south-east of Worksop on the A1. If driving south-east from the Worksop area you will need to be ready to get into the right-hand lane of the A1 dual carriageway to cross into Elkesley.*

THE PUB

The staff of the **Robin Hood Inn** have got it exactly right. They're friendly, welcoming, polite and courteous. How many times can you say that nowadays? Like quite a few Nottinghamshire pubs, though, there is only one cask ale available and that is Black Sheep Bitter. They also sell a smooth beer, as well as lager and cider so I am sure you will find something that quenches your thirst. There's a large and excellent menu with main dishes such as crisp confit duck leg, Oriental greens, soy, sesame and chilli. If you fancy something slightly less exotic, then what about fried scampi, chips, garden peas, salad and tartare sauce? There is a specials board which, when I was there, included both leek and potato soup with croutons, as well as chicken curry, rice, mango chutney and poppadoms. There are also sandwiches and snacks and I can thoroughly recommend the Lincolnshire sausage and onion in a baguette – delicious after a walk on a cool autumn day.

Opening times are Tuesday to Saturday 11.30 am until 2 pm and

6 pm until 11 pm; and on Sunday from 12 noon until 4 pm.
☎ *01777 838259*

1 With your back to the **Robin Hood Inn** turn right along the road, passing the church on your left. Keep on through the village, ignoring the road to the A1 on the right. Turn left along **Headland Avenue**. Fork right along **Lawnwood Lane**. At a T-junction with a track, turn right along the tarmac lane. Pass **Twin Oaks** on your right. Ignore the track to the left after this. Ignore another lane to the right. Keep on towards the large metal building ahead and walk down the right side of it on a bridleway. It's huge! At the end of the building bear right, then left and descend to the entrance of a yard.

2 Cross the road at the entrance to the yard and immediately bear left along a rougher track. In 100 yards you reach a ford and a bridge over the **River Poulter**. Keep forward beyond this with private woods on both sides. After 300 yards, where the track swings left, fork right for 40 yards, then left along the bridleway below the electricity lines. At the edge of the wood, walk forward, still along the line of electricity poles.

3 On reaching a track, cross straight over. The track rises gently. On reaching some buildings on your left, turn left passing the nearest one on your right. Follow the path with the hedge on your right to the end of the field. Keep in the same direction in the second field, with the hedge on your right as before. In the third field, keep the hedge on your right for 15 yards, bearing slightly left up the field aiming just to the left of the small wood at the top of the field. The wood is on an ancient motte.

Fungi in Elkesley Wood

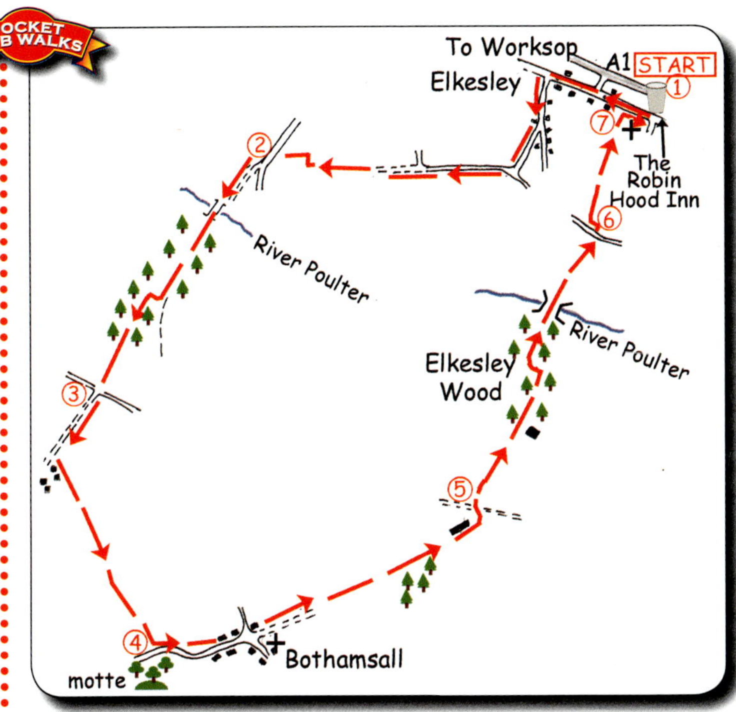

4 Turn left when you reach the road, taking care at the bottom of the hill where the road narrows for just a few yards. Walk through **Bothamsall** to reach the church. Walk along **Church Lane** to the left of the church. It is marked as a dead-end but you can walk through beyond it. Keep forward ignoring all tracks off it. Pass **Fourwinds** on your right. Pass through a bridlegate, proceeding alongside a hedge on your right. Pass through a farm gate now with a hedge on your left and a wood a field away to your right. Where the wood ends to your right, keep forward to pass through a farm gate and follow the track towards the buildings ahead. When you reach the end of the redbrick buildings turn left along the track and keep all remaining buildings to your left.

Keep forward with the farmyard on your left and a hedge on your right. Pass through a bridlegate by a farm gate.

5 Cross to the track ahead of you. It is private to left and right. Beyond the track, bear slightly right towards a property ahead. As the track swings right to the house, bear slightly left into **Elkesley Wood** just beyond. Some 200 yards after entering the wood, the path splits. Turn left here and 60 yards later go right as the path splits again. On joining a more vague track coming in from the left, bear right. The path then forks, both paths leading to a footbridge over the **River Poulter**, which you crossed earlier. Walk up the path in the field ahead to reach a track.

6 Turn left here for 10 yards then turn right down the side of a field. When the hedge on your right ends, keep forward. Towards the end of the field keep on along the tarmac path. On reaching a road walk along it to reach another road. Turn left here, then right into **Beech Walk**. Keep straight ahead on this, and the path at the end, to reach the main village road.

7 Turn right, back to the **Robin Hood Inn**.

Places of interest nearby

The Cheetham family make their Thaymar ice cream at **Haughton Park House Farm** which is one mile south-east of Elkesley off the B6387. ☎ 01623 862632. If you haven't got time to visit, the ice cream is available if you follow Walk 3 from Worksop – the little kiosk at Turnerwood Cottage on the Chesterfield Canal sells it. There is also **Thoresby Gallery** near Ollerton which is now a retail centre. You might pick up some bargain walking clothes! ☎ 01623 822365

5 Edwinstowe

The Forest Lodge Hotel

The sun always shines in Edwinstowe. I know it sounds unlikely but every time I visit it does. If you are as lucky as me, then walking beneath the trees of Sherwood Forest, with the sun peeping through the foliage, will help shine away the stresses and strains of our modern lives. Edwinstowe is where Robin Hood married Maid Marian and although you don't pass the Major Oak on the walk it isn't far off if you want to look at it and it should be signposted. King Edwin of Northumbria was killed nearby, in the 7th century, and his body was buried here, hence the name of Edwinstowe.

Distance – 5¼ miles

OS Explorer 270 Sherwood Forest GR 625672

A chance to explore Sherwood Forest. Once you've left Edwinstowe and the area around the Major Oak you will find yourself getting away from the crowds. They don't know what they're missing.

Starting point The car park near the Art & Craft Centre in Edwinstowe.

How to get there *Enter Edwinstowe from the west on the A6075. Turn left at the crossroads (passing the Forest Lodge Hotel as you go). After 250 yards turn left towards the Sherwood Forest Art & Craft Centre.*

THE PUB

The **Forest Lodge Hotel** has a bar area where you can have a good meal if the restaurant is not open. The bar meals have always been really enjoyable when I have been there. They could include dishes such as chicken sizzler stir fry and gammon with an egg or pineapple. There are also omelettes, salads and sandwiches. Then there's the specials board which might include home-made moussaka, vegetable stir fry or tuna on a bed of stir-fried vegetables. The regular beers are Bombardier with four guests such as Young's Bitter, Outlaw Brewing Co's Wrangler and Acorn Brewery's Forester.

Bar meals are available from 12 noon until 2 pm and from 6 pm until 9 pm every day. ☎ *01623 824443*

1 From the car park walk back to the B6034. On reaching the road turn left. Follow the bridleway with the road on your right. Keep just right of the cricket ground and rise up the gravel path. At a crossroads of paths, keep straight ahead. At another crossroads,

keep forward. On reaching a wide fenced path cross this, keeping forward for a third time. At a fourth crossroads, turn left to have a look at the Major Oak but make sure you return to keep in the same direction as before. You come out into the open. Keep forward ignoring paths and tracks to left and right. At another crossroads keep straight on. On reaching a gravel track keep forward (bearing slightly left). Again you're out in the open. You reach a point with a cattle grid to left and right. Walk on towards the trees ahead along a stony track.

2 On reaching the edge of the heathland you have just crossed, walk out onto the gravel track and turn left. (Ignore tracks to the right and straight ahead.) Proceed beside **Ladysmith Plantation** on your right and **Budby South Forest** on your left. (You will have left Sherwood Forest National Nature Reserve behind.) At the end of the wood on your right there are fields beyond.

In Sherwood Forest

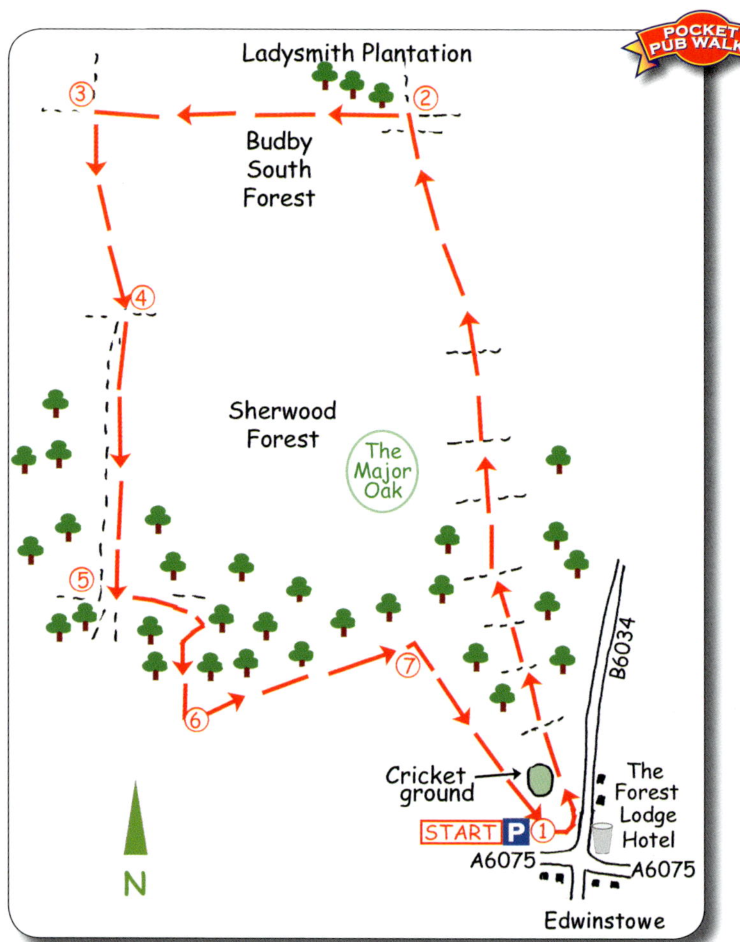

3 On reaching a staggered crossroads of tracks, turn left for **Centre Tree**. **Budby South Forest** is still on your left. Ignore tracks to left and right. The track begins to rise. Then it forks. Bear *slightly* right here, ignoring the track to the left.

4 You reach another crossroads. Turn left here for a couple of yards or so before turning right to walk along a grassy bridleway in the same direction as before – the gravel track should be running parallel to you on your right. Ignore a path on your left into the forest. The bridleway begins to rise again.

5 When the bridleway levels out various tracks come together and there is a large oak tree here. Is this Centre Tree? Turn left here along a slightly narrower path. After 60 yards fork right for **Edwinstowe**. This is a 'real' footpath, about a foot wide! In 300 yards at a crossroads of paths turn right and 100 yards later the path swings left. (Ignore the path going straight ahead.) Follow the path to reach the bridleway just inside the edge of the wood.

6 Turn left along the bridleway for ¾ mile.

7 On joining a bridleway coming in from the left, turn right staying just inside the forest with fields on your right. Keep to the right of the cricket ground to come back to the craft centre and the car park.

Places of interest nearby

You could visit the visitor centre at **Sherwood Forest Country Park**, just north of Edwinstowe between points 1 and 2, either afterwards or as you walk by. ☎ 01623 823202. Then there is **St Mary's church** in Edwinstowe where Robin Hood married Maid Marian – you might want to check to see if it is open. ☎ 01623 822430. Finally there is the **Sherwood Forest Art & Craft Centre** in Edwinstowe. ☎ 01623 824976

6 Laxton

The Dovecote Inn

It's hard to know where to start with Laxton. I've never seen so many farmhouses on a village street. Surrounding the village is an open field system and the earthworks of a castle built 800 years ago. What is wonderful about the open field system is that it is being used even now by local farmers. It is a real living museum, and that is perhaps how it should be.

THE PUB

The **Dovecote Inn** is even better now than when I last visited it four or five years ago – and I really liked it back then. They provide 'traditional pub food with a twist'. It is all locally sourced and fresh. Let me mention, before I forget, that on Monday, at lunchtime from 12 noon until 2 pm, there's a fish and chip special on offer. There are also hot baguettes and sandwiches available with the bacon and brie being very popular,

Distance – 4½ miles

OS Explorer 271 Newark-on-Trent GR 724671

Laxton is unique – a last remnant of a medieval style of life. With its ancient open field system you can follow the footpaths through Mill Field and almost see some of the agricultural workers who used to work here. One word of warning – mud. If it has been wet there could be some!

Starting point The visitor centre car park behind the Dovecote Inn in Laxton.

How to get there *Laxton is 3 miles or so east of Ollerton. As you drive through the village you can't miss the Dovecote Inn.*

as well as tuna mayonnaise. The main meals include dishes like slow-roast belly pork and Lancashire hotpot. You might be paying slightly more than you would in some pubs but it is well worth it in my estimation. There are always three guest beers on sale such as Orkney's Dark Island, Wooden Hand's Cornish Buccaneer and Robinson's Wags to Witches.

Food is available from Monday to Saturday 12 noon until 2 pm and from 6.30 pm until 9 pm; and on Sunday from 12.30 pm until 6.30 pm. ☎ 01777 871586

1 Walk back to the road from the car park and turn right. Walk up the hill keeping to the left of the grass triangle, turning left along the road for **Boughton** and **Ollerton**. When you reach the end of the churchyard on your left, turn right along the bridleway. It can be muddy. Some 300 yards later, swing left along the grassy path but before you do, look straight ahead into the field to see the remains of **Laxton Castle**, a medieval castle built by the Norman landowner Robert de Caux.

The copse at point 4 of the walk

2 Having turned left, proceed for 450 yards along the grassy path. Climb a stile at the end of the green lane, then another stile immediately on your left. Walk alongside a hedge on your right. Part way along, the path bears slightly left towards the corner of a hedge jutting out into the field. Beyond this walk down to the lane. Turn right opposite **Top Farm** along the tarmac road. Keep straight forward through the double gate where the lane ends and a track swings right. In 100 yards fork left along a narrower hedged path. After 300 yards cross a lane, carefully.

3 Walk along the gravel track ahead. Ignore a track that crosses it. Keep forward at the crossroads of paths where you may find an interpretation panel. This is **Mill Field**, the largest of the open fields in the village. According to the interpretation panel, in 1635 it contained 833 acres but now there are only 196. This is largely a treeless area and, as you go, you will see the different strips of land with no hedges or walls separating them. The track loses height and becomes grassier. Where the track forks, take the right fork which becomes a wide green lane, ten or so yards wide. The lane narrows and you cross a stream. Then the green lane rises and you pass under the electricity lines strung between pylons. The path straightens and rises straight uphill.

4 After the path levels out to some extent, turn sharp left through a gateway on your left. Walk towards the gap on the far side of the field, aiming for the pylon nearest the farm across the fields. On reaching the gap pass through the smaller of the two gaps that are actually there. Walk alongside the hedge on your right. At the bottom of the field turn left (inside the field) walking alongside a ditch on your right. Cross a concrete bridge on your right and turn left immediately, walking alongside the same hedge you were following before. Pass through a gap in the hedge with the same

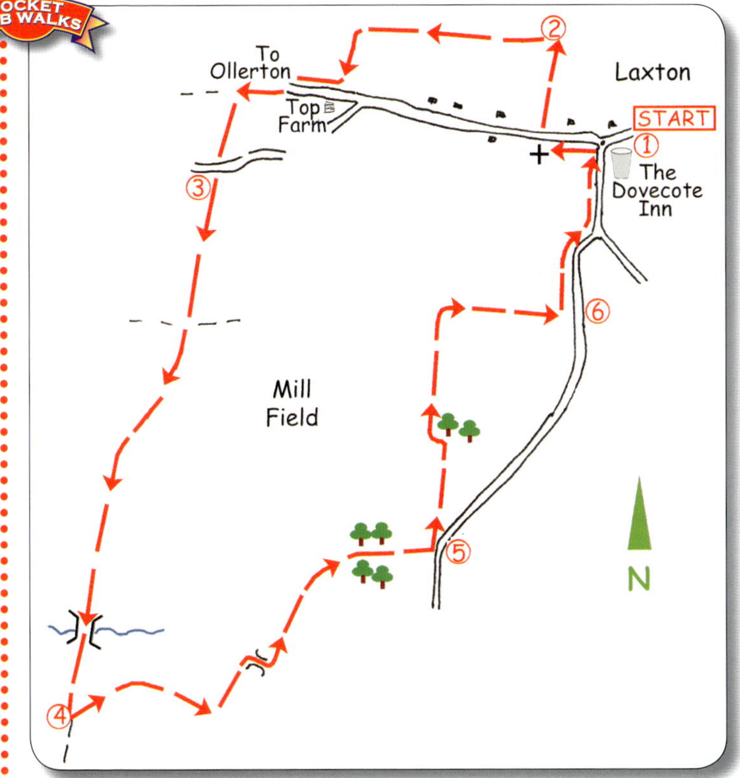

ditch (but no hedge) still on your left. Bear half right and walk towards the copse of trees on the far side of the field. Keep to the right of the nearest electricity pylon. Cross another bridge and cut across the corner of the next field, passing through the copse of trees some 30 yards from the corner of the field. On the far side of the trees, keep straight forward across the field to pass through a gap in the hedge to reach a lane.

5 Turn left immediately up a track between hedges. Keep on the right-hand side of the field when the track swings left into the field. The path rises and then descends into the corner of a field. Turn left here, inside the field, to walk beside some trees on your right. After 80 yards (at the end of the trees) swing right and walk beside a hedge on your right. You are now back in **Mill Field**. After 300 yards the hedge ends at a T-junction of paths. Turn right along a grassy path. Keep right to descend into the trees and bushes as the path runs along a sunken lane. Follow the path through the trees. Pass through a gate, walking forward through a muddy area. Note the parallel 'furrows', created over the years by cows walking through here.

6 At the lane, turn left back towards **Laxton**. After 300 yards, ignore a lane from the right, keep ahead, back into **Laxton** and to the **Dovecote Inn** on your right.

Places of interest nearby

The **Holocaust Centre** on the outskirts of Laxton provides a poignant contrast to our freedom to wander the fields of Nottinghamshire at will. ☎ 01623 836627. South of Ollerton, **Rufford Abbey** is worth exploring and is one of Nottinghamshire's most popular attractions. ☎ 01623 821338. Don't forget to have a good look around the small **Visitor Centre at Laxton** too.

7 Teversal

The Teversal Grange Country Inn

There is a fair chance that cyclists will outnumber walkers on the Teversal Trail but it's too good a walking opportunity to miss. At times you're below the level of the surrounding ground ... at others you rise above it. There are one or two places where you can sit and watch the world go by – this might comprise the occasional cock pheasant wandering past and that will be about it. The small village of Teversal might surprise you, in particular St Katherine's church and churchyard. The stonework surrounding one of the church doors is really unusual comprising symbols that are supposed to represent St Katherine's life.

Distance – 4 miles

OS Explorer 269 Chesterfield & Alfreton GR 479613

A level walk following a couple of the local trails that have been created on disused railway lines. This is a surprisingly lush and leafy area in spring and summer.

Starting point The car park between the visitor centre and Teversal Grange Country Inn.

How to get there *Follow the signs for the Teversal Trail Visitor Centre on the B6014 between Tibshelf and Skegby.*

THE PUB

The **Teversal Grange Country Inn** sits between the visitor centre and the cricket pitch, and the football ground is only a stone's throw away too. It is quite a large, friendly pub. The regular beer is Black Sheep bitter with three guest beers which could include Shepherd Neame's Bishops Finger, Palmers Dorset Gold and Batemans Middle Wicket. The Teversal Grange has a carvery each day which usually includes a choice of three different meats. Then there are main meals such as hot roast beef bap and chips, lasagne classic, as well as crispy-coated fish medley. The same family has run the Teversal Grange Country Inn for over 20 years. They must be doing something right.

Opening times during the week are from 11.30 am until 3 pm and from 5 pm until 11 pm; on Saturday from 12 noon until 4 pm and from 6.30 pm until midnight; and on Sunday from 11.30 am until 3 pm and from 6 pm until 10.30 pm. ☎ *01623 441017*

1 With your back to the visitor centre turn left towards the **Teversal Coal Garden**. Look out for the red and black winding wheel halves. Follow the gravel path through the garden. Pass through a kissing gate, ignore the path forking left and keep forward to a T-junction

to reach the Trail. Turn left for **Tibshelf**, 3 miles away. After passing through a fence turn right for **Silverhill Wood** and **Pleasley**.

Teversal village

2 On reaching a bridge over a road, keep forward along the Trail. Just beyond the bridge, ignore the left fork for **Silverhill Wood**, keeping straight forward for **Pleasley**, 2 miles away. A delightful stretch of walking ensues. Pass under a rather high redbrick bridge. Pass under another bridge. The Trail subsequently rises steeply to a lane.

3 Turn right for a few yards before turning left, descending back to the Trail. Proceed along the deep cutting for nearly ¾ mile. You pass out of Nottinghamshire, into Derbyshire on your way. You reach a point where you turn left (towards the **Rowthorne Trail**). Turn right after a few yards to descend to **Batley Lane**. Take care in case cars are passing by. Turn right for 200 yards along the lane.

4 Turn right on reaching the Trail, for **Skegby**. You pass back into Nottinghamshire. The Trail crosses a bridge over a road. You then pass under a rather ramshackle metal bridge. Cross another bridge over farmland. Some 20 yards before reaching a pair of wooden electricity poles, turn right down the steps of a public footpath. On reaching a tunnel to your left, turn right through

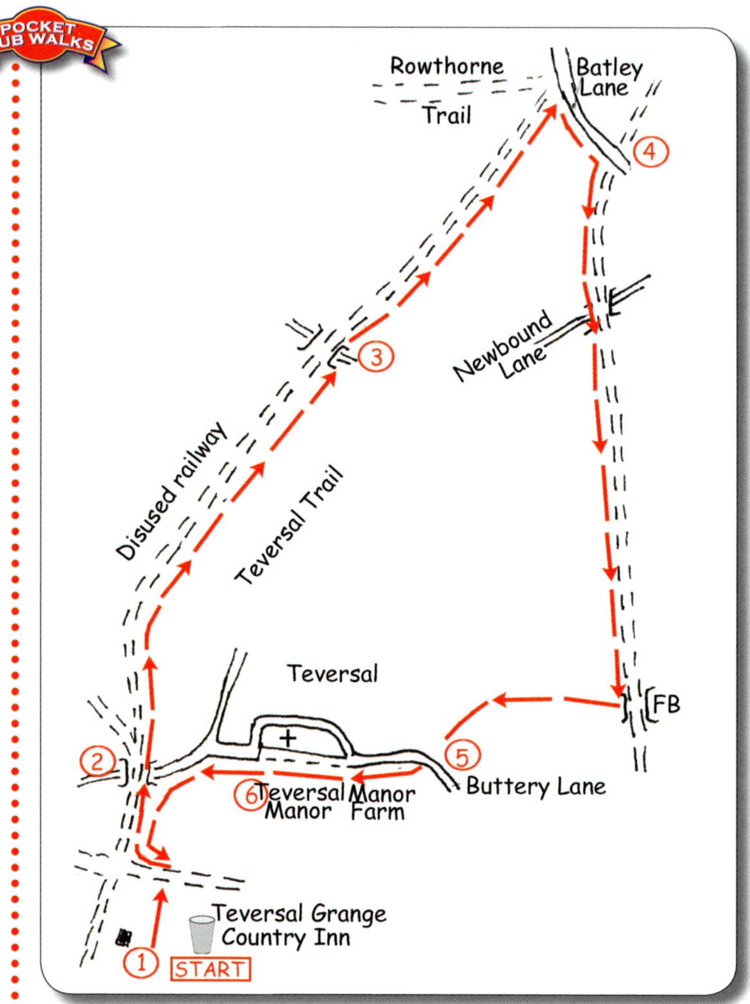

a kissing gate. Bear right for 10 yards to cross a step-over stile. Walk up the right side of the field with electricity lines above your head. Most people walk up the right side of the field to the top right corner before turning left within the field to reach **Buttery Lane**. (The OS map appears to show that you should cut across the top right corner of the field.)

5 On the lane bear right for 250 yards to reach **Teversal** village. Where the lane bends right (with a footpath on your left) keep straight forward along the driveway between buildings. Pass **Manor Farm** on your left. Go through a kissing gate beside a larger gate. It is worth exploring the church and churchyard on your right. Continue along the lane passing **Teversal Manor** on your left, ignoring the driveway leading away from it to the right. Keep forward as the path you are on narrows and brings you to the road.

6 Keep forward along the road along an avenue of trees. On reaching another road, ignore the right turn for Pleasley. Keep forward for **Sutton-in-Ashfield**. The road descends and you reach bridge 15TSC passing over the road. Climb up the steps back onto the Trail. Turn left for Teversal visitor centre. Take the next left still signed for the visitor centre and then turn right, back to your car.

Places of interest nearby

Head north a few miles to visit the National Trust property, **Hardwick Hall** – surely one of the most impressive of stately homes. ☎ 01246 850430. **Hardwick Old Hall** is right next door which is truly fascinating in its own way. If you don't like heights though you may want to stay at ground level. ☎ 01246 850431. **Stainsby Mill** is only a mile or so away from both halls. ☎ 01246 850430. Near to Hardwick Hall, at Ault Hucknall, is **St John the Baptist church,** on the side of which is an ancient carving of St George and the dragon. ☎ 01246 850371

8 Ravenshead

The Hutt

The Robin Hood Way runs through the woodland to the north of Ravenshead. In fact, you follow it for a couple of miles so look out for the small waymarks with a bow and arrow pointing out its course. The walk also passes through Thieves' Wood which allegedly refers to the sort of people who would be awaiting the unwary traveller. There is also the option of cutting out two miles of the route by taking a short cut back to Ravenshead but then you would miss out seeing the site where, famously, Friar Tuck carried Robin Hood across a stream before dumping him, unceremoniously, into the water.

Distance – 7½ miles

OS Explorer 270 Sherwood Forest GR 556543

A bit of a different walk this, with some roadside walking (on pavements) at the beginning and end. In between though there's lovely countryside and, of course, Robin Hood is never far away.

Starting point The car park of The Hutt.

How to get there *The Hutt is opposite the entrance to Newstead Abbey on the A60 in Ravenshead.*

THE PUB

My companion on the day we visited **The Hutt** commented on the way that all the staff were so polite and courteous. The Hutt is a Chef and Brewer and although some frown upon pubs in a chain we have always really enjoyed the food served here. There is certainly plenty of choice with dishes from the 'pub classics' section of the menu comprising Moroccan spiced lamb burgers, hand-battered fish and Indonesian curry. Then there is a sharers' section if two of you want to dip into a meal together. This includes meze, seafood and antipasti platters. I'm only scratching the surface though, as there are also chicken dishes, fish dishes, as well as starters and steaks. Beer-wise there are usually three regulars such as Bombardier, Courage Directors and Marston's Pedigree. The guests vary every week and could include JW Lees Scorcher amongst others.

Opening times are Monday to Thursday from 11 am until 11 pm; Friday and Saturday from 11 am until 11.30 pm; and on Sunday from 11 am until 10.30 pm. ☎ 01623 792325

1 From **The Hutt**, walk north along the A60 towards Mansfield. Use the pelican crossing to walk along the left side of this busy road.

2 Half a mile later turn left along the **Kirkby road** after using the pelican crossing to walk on the right side of the road. Ignore a lane to the right. In 600 yards turn right down a lane towards the woodland. At the bottom of the hill (on a left-hand bend) take the footpath into **Thieves' Wood**. Keep forward, ignoring paths to left and right. At an interpretation panel where five paths meet (with a car park to your left) keep forward. Cross a track, rising slightly. On reaching a sandy track, turn right for 175 yards.

The path through Thieves' Wood

3 Turn right on another track, keeping straight ahead when the track bends right. Ignore all cross paths as you proceed. Your path swings left slightly and you gradually lose height. The path eventually rises uphill slightly. Ahead you may hear the cars on the A60.

4 At the A60 turn right for 200 yards. Turn left along the bridleway (25 yards before a track into the wood). Follow the bridleway directly away from the road to reach another track. Turn right along this following the **Robin Hood Way**. Stay on this, ignoring a narrow path that crosses it. Ignore another path to the left. Where the **Robin Hood Way** forks, take the right fork.

5 *For the short cut, turn right at a crossroads of paths and follow the directions from point 7.* Otherwise, at the crossroads, keep ahead along the **Robin Hood Way**. At an interpretation panel you will see you are in **Fountain Dale** where Friar Tuck carried Robin Hood across a stream. Ignore a path to the left here. With open fields on your left, stay just inside the wood. On reaching the end

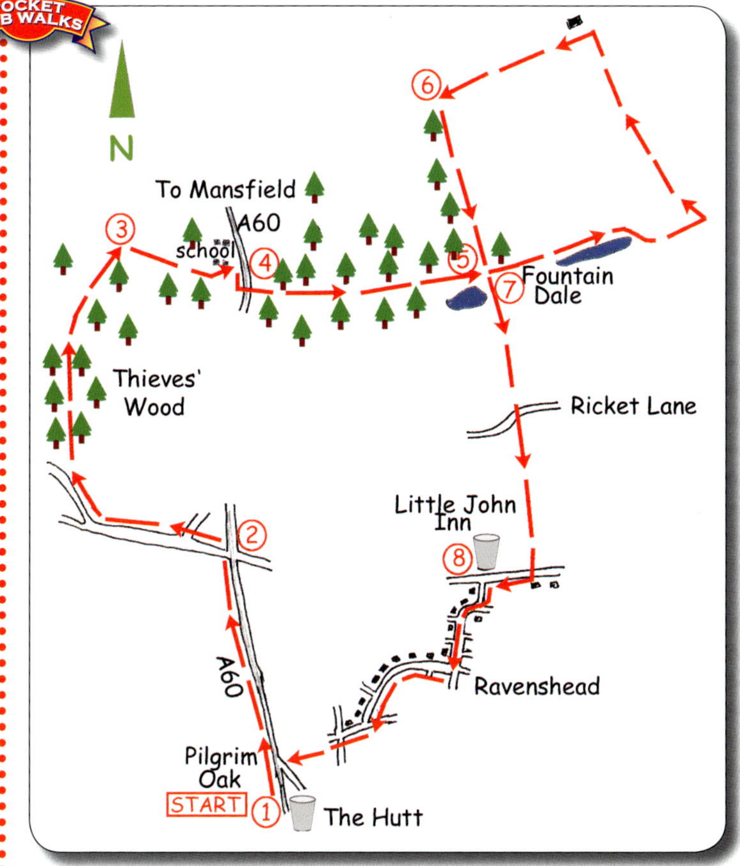

of a pond on your right, swing left into the fields along a low concrete 'bridge'. Keep forward with the wood on your right. Enter a second field. On reaching a crossroads of bridleways in the third field, turn sharp left to walk towards the hedgerow 100 yards away. Walk up between the double hedgerows for half a mile. On reaching **Lindhurst Farm**, turn left along a gravel track with the farm buildings on your right. Keep forward for 500 yards.

6 At the edge of the wood turn left down another bridleway. Ignore all paths to your right. When the bridleway forks (and with a path to your right) keep forward along the middle of three paths. After 250 yards you come back to the crossroads with the **Robin Hood Way**.

7 Cross this, heading forward. The bridleway leaves the wood and runs between hedges. Cross quiet **Ricket Lane**. Walk forward beyond. Ignore all paths to the left. At a driveway, keep forward once again.

8 At the road, turn right towards the **Little John Inn**. Just beyond, turn left along **Bretton Road**. Swing right at the T-junction, then left into **Hereford Road**. This rises uphill. Ignore all roads to left and right. Eventually, turn right into **Swinton Rise**. Again ignore all roads off it. At a T-junction turn right (ignoring a footpath opposite) to reach **Sheepwalk Lane** 150 yards later. Cross this bearing slightly left to follow the footpath to the left of **Pilgrim Close**. This brings you back to **The Hutt**.

Place of interest nearby

The obvious nearby place to suggest is of course **Newstead Abbey**, the home of Lord Byron at the beginning of the 19th century. You could have another leisurely stroll after you've had lunch in The Hutt perhaps. ☎ 01623 455900

9 Farnsfield

The Plough Inn

Something like two-fifths of this walk is along the Southwell Trail. It's not far off being a straight couple of miles either but with the trees on either side it is never tedious. In autumn the colours merit a steady strolling pace along here whilst in summer the dappled light will surely enthral you and the leaves will keep you cool on even the hottest of days. On the way back you pass through the fields surrounding Cotton Mill Farm before following one of those charming hedged village paths which brings you back to the pub before you realise.

Distance – 4¼ miles

OS Explorer 270 Sherwood Forest GR 649565

There are no hills on this fascinating walk linking the villages of Farnsfield and Edingley along the Southwell Trail which is lovely at any time of year.

Starting point The pub car park (let them know) or on the road known as The Ridgeway which is a road near the Plough Inn.

How to get there *Farnsfield is to the east of Mansfield, south of the A617 between Mansfield and Newark-on-Trent. The Plough Inn is on the main street in the village.*

THE PUB

The **Plough Inn** is a traditional village pub. It always seems lively and long may it last. It's cosy and has oak beams and is everything a pub should be. There is a healthy choice of beers, with regulars such as Marston's Original Bitter and Mansfield's Smooth Creamy Ale on offer. There are also guests such as Brakspear's Oxford Gold, Jennings Cocker Hoop and Marston's Pomp and Circumstance. There is plenty of variety on the menu too. Main courses comprise chilli con carne, gammon egg and chips and cheese omelette. There are light bites such as meat salad, cheese salad, ploughman's lunch and chip cob. I am assured June's home-made pies are very popular whether you try the chicken and mushroom pie, the steak and kidney pie or the meat and potato pie. One small point, walkers – if you're wet and muddy, could you please use the Tap Room.

Opening times are 11 am to 11 pm, with food served from noon until 2 pm. Food is also available from 5.30 pm to 7.30 pm Monday to Friday. ☎ *01623 882265*

1 With your back to the **Plough**, turn left along **Main Street** and swing left along **The Ridgeway**. Stay on this ignoring all roads to left and right. After 1/3 mile, with **D'Ayncourt Walk** on your left, the road swings right. Keep forward though, walking along the path past houses 2 to 10 on your left. This brings you to the **Southwell Trail**.

2 Turn right, making sure you walk along the path nearest the fields. Stay on this for 1½ miles. Ignore all paths crossing it. This is delightful, especially in autumn. Some 80 yards before a small car park turn sharp right down some steps. There is an interpretation panel at the car park if you want to learn more about the Trail. Walk along the left side of the first field. **Edingley Beck** is in the ditch on your left. Stay on the left side of a second, a third and then a fourth field. At the end of the fourth field, bear slightly right to cross a gravel track. Stay on the left side of the subsequent fields, still beside the beck. About 50 yards before you reach the main street through **Edingley**, with a footbridge on your left, turn half right across the field towards the side of a brick building.

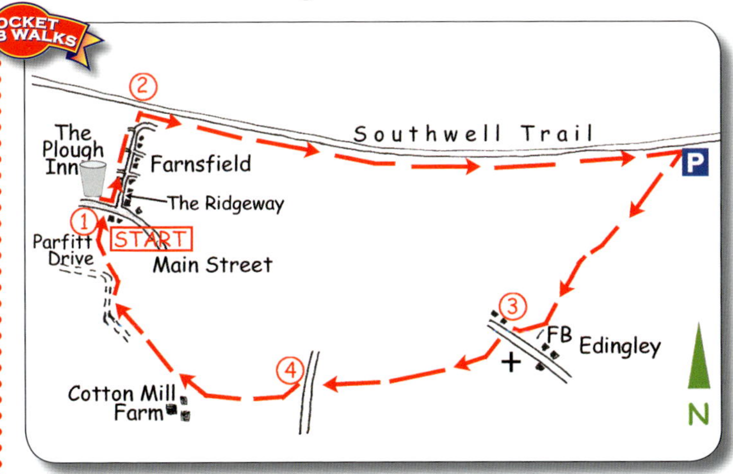

3 Turn right on the road for 15 yards then left along a track running alongside the churchyard. Before reaching the houses, turn right through a metal gate. Walk across the field and pass through a gap. Bear slightly left over a footbridge. Head across the field beyond towards another metal gate. Keep forward in the fourth and fifth fields. Pass through another kissing gate and follow the gravel track. Ignore the entrance to a property on your left, keeping forward with a hedge on your left. Go through a gap at the end of the field, keeping in the same direction to reach a narrow country lane. Take care crossing it.

4 Cross the footbridge and walk along the left side of the field, with another ditch on your left. Bear right inside the field still with the ditch on your left. Stay on the left side of a second field. Turn right at a farm track, passing the brick buildings of **Cotton Mill Farm** on your left. At the end of these buildings (with a house on your right) bear left to a bridlegate. Walk along the right side of the field beyond towards the spire of **Farnsfield church** ahead. Climb the stiles beside a pair of gates. Proceed along the track with the sports field on your left. At the end of this turn right on the track. As the track swings left, fork right onto a gravel path through the hedge. This leads to a new housing development called **Parfitt Drive**, named after the pilot of a Halifax bomber that crashed near here in 1944 killing all seven airmen onboard. Keep forward to follow the hedged path straight ahead. This leads to a staggered crossroads of paths. Keep right here, ignoring both paths to the left. Progress along the narrow path between hedgerows, then walls. This brings you back to the **Plough Inn**.

On the Southwell Trail

Places of interest nearby

White Post Farm just west of Farnsfield is ideal for children who may like to see and meet some of the farm animals. ☎ 01623 882977. There is, of course, **Southwell Minster** – even if you don't go inside, just walk round it. ☎ 01636 812649. **Southwell Workhouse,** a National Trust property, gives an insight into how the poor souls who lived there suffered in the 19th century. ☎ 01636 817260

10 Farndon

The Rose & Crown

Most walkers have an unhealthy interest in the different types of stile and gates they climb over or pass through ... or is it just me? Well, on this walk you'll see a couple of fine examples of the clapper gate. I've only ever seen them beside the River Trent and the ones around Farndon have actually had a lick of paint! Now it's not just the clapper gates that you can look forward to ... there are the redbrick houses and the church in the old part of Farndon; there's the path alongside the River Trent; and the wildfowl at Averham Weir – even Staythorpe power station across the river has its own merits.

Distance – 3½ miles

OS Explorer 271 Newark-on-Trent GR 769517

Probably the flattest walk in the book. Take your binoculars as there is often plenty of wildfowl at Averham Weir.

Starting point The car park behind the Rose & Crown, or on the road nearby.

How to get there *Drive south on the A46 out of Newark. Ignore the right turn for 'Farndon Marina', take the next right for 'Farndon'. The Rose & Crown is along this road on the left.*

THE PUB The **Rose & Crown** is a community pub and the staff genuinely friendly. If you want a glass of beer after your walk, then on offer are Everard's Beacon, Tiger and Original plus a guest such as Everard's Scorcher. Good wholesome pub food such as lasagne, lamb shank, sausage and mash, liver and bacon, as well as cottage pie is on offer – the sort of food you need if it has been a bit on the cool side whilst you were walking beside the River Trent. At lunchtimes there are also hot crusty baguettes available filled with cheddar cheese, or tuna mayonnaise or prawn and Marie Rose sauce.

Opening times are Monday from 4 pm until midnight; Tuesday from 12 noon until 11 pm; Wednesday to Sunday from 12 noon until midnight. ☎ *01636 704334*

1 With your back to the front of the **Rose & Crown**, turn left along the road. Ignore a road to the left (Cross Lane) and then a left fork (Church Street). Ignore Marsh Lane to the right. After 125 yards turn right along a footpath between houses. On reaching a lane, turn left before turning right along **North End**. Ignore a path to your left and a road to the right. As **North End** swings

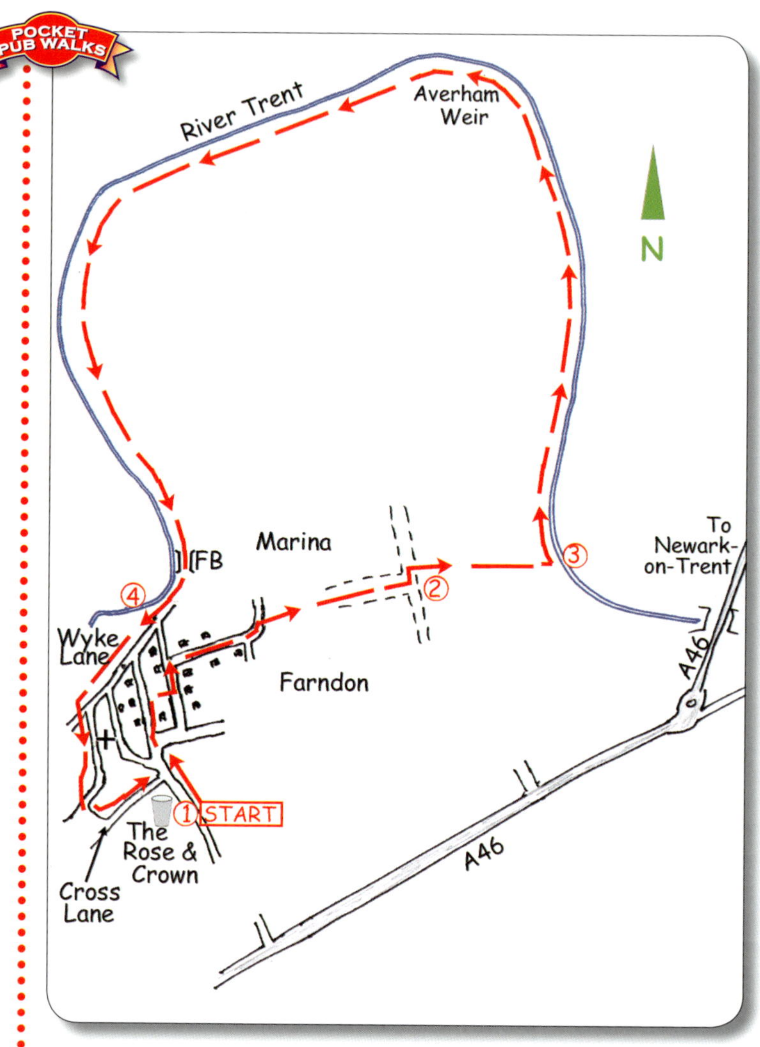
POCKET PUB WALKS
River Trent
Averham Weir
N
Marina
FB
To Newark-on-Trent
Wyke Lane
Farndon
A46
START
The Rose & Crown
Cross Lane
A46

The River Trent

left, take the footpath on your right through a gap in the wall. Walk between two rows of garages. Keep forward into an open area. Walk to the far left corner passing **Farndon Marina** on your left. Pass through a kissing gate, keeping forward along the gravel track ahead (ignoring another to your left).

2 On reaching a T-junction of tracks, turn left for 60 yards. Then cross a stile on your right and walk to the far end of a smallholding. Cross another stile, following the clear path through the rougher ground towards the far right corner. Beyond this aim half right towards the bridge taking the A46 over the **River Trent**. Proceed

towards this to reach the river. Do not pass through the clapper gate to your right.

3 Turn left alongside the **Trent** passing plenty of fishermen's numbered pegs. Eventually, after passing through a clapper gate beside the river, you reach a turning circle. Keep on the tarmac track beyond, still beside the river. You reach **Averham Weir** where there is often a lot of bird life. I saw great crested grebes, a cormorant, geese, ducks, swans and a heron. Stay beside the river when the track bears left. Staythorpe power station is on your right, you won't miss it. The track stays beside the river but starts to bear left as the river does. A newly-planted wood is reached but ignore all paths to your left. Keep beside the river to reach and cross a striking metal bridge with **Farndon Marina** on your left. Stay on the path passing the premises of the 6th Newark Sea Scout Group on your left. Walk past a picnic area and through the car park of **Farndon Boathouse Bar & Kitchen** and the car park beyond that. Bear right along **Wyke Lane**.

4 After 50 yards, fork right (still along Wyke Lane). Pass **Farndon Willow Holt Nature Reserve** on your right. Ignore the first lane on your left but take the second one to pass **St Peter's church** on your left. The lane bends right. On reaching another road, swing left into **Cross Lane** to reach the pub.

Places of interest nearby

If you don't know **Newark-on-Trent** you should have a walk round. There is **Newark Castle** to explore, ☎ 01636 655765, as well as nearby **Millgate Museum** with its displays of life in the 19th and 20th centuries. ☎ 01636 655735. Just outside the town is **Newark Air Museum** which their website describes as 'one of the UK's largest volunteer managed aviation museums'. ☎ 01636 707170

11 Bleasby

The Waggon and Horses

Look at the Ordnance Survey map of this area and you will see that there is nearly as much water as land between Bleasby and Hoveringham. Be prepared therefore if there has been heavy rain to encounter some mud or, even worse, flooding. In the latter case you will have to walk elsewhere or, before you leave home, check the position online. Both villages are delightful and quiet. Whilst passing through Bleasby, near the pub, look out for Borrow Bread Lane – now I wonder how that name came about?

Distance – 6¼ miles

OS Explorer 260 Nottingham GR 716496

Nothing too testing on this half-day's walk linking the attractive villages of Bleasby and Hoveringham. It may be a little muddy on the way back.

Starting point The car park of the Waggon and Horses.

How to get there *Bleasby is north-east of Nottingham. Drive along the A612 from Lowdham. Turn right for Bleasby in Thurgarton, then a mile or more later, right into Station Road. Stay on this road to enter Bleasby. The Waggon and Horses is on your left just before the church. The car park is behind the pub and there is limited parking in front.*

THE PUB

The **Waggon and Horses** is one of the most attractive pubs from the outside, a real country pub. It's attractive inside too, with a marvellous choice of food and drink.

The beers are really interesting as the pub uses the smaller breweries rather than the big names. For instance, there are always two beers from Blue Monkey Brewery such as Orginal, Evolution or BG Sips. Then there might be Abbeydale's Daily Bread or Oldershaw's First Class. The chef was keen to point out that as many ingredients as possible are locally sourced so on the specials board you could have Trent Valley marbled fillet steak then, from slightly further afield, cod mornay or fresh Cornish scallops. The Sunday roast is recommended with perhaps a choice of topside of beef or hand-reared pork. On the regular menu there are traditional pub dishes like home-made steak and real ale pie, Bleasby bangers and mash and beer battered cod with minted peas. Sandwiches are also available using locally sourced fresh bread from Farnsfield.

Food is served from 12 noon until 2.30 pm and from 5.30 pm until 8.30 pm though there is no food available on Monday or Tuesday.
☎ 01636 830283

1 With your back to the front of the pub, turn right along the short stretch of lane then turn left past **St Mary's church**. At the crossroads keep forward along **Boat Lane** for **Hazelford**. Just before a left-hand bend ignore a footpath on your right. Just on the bend though (and before a right-hand bend) take the footpath on your right over a two-plank bridge. Walk directly towards the gable ends of the property on the far side of the field. At the far side pass through a gap and turn left to the road. Turn right to walk down to the **River Trent**.

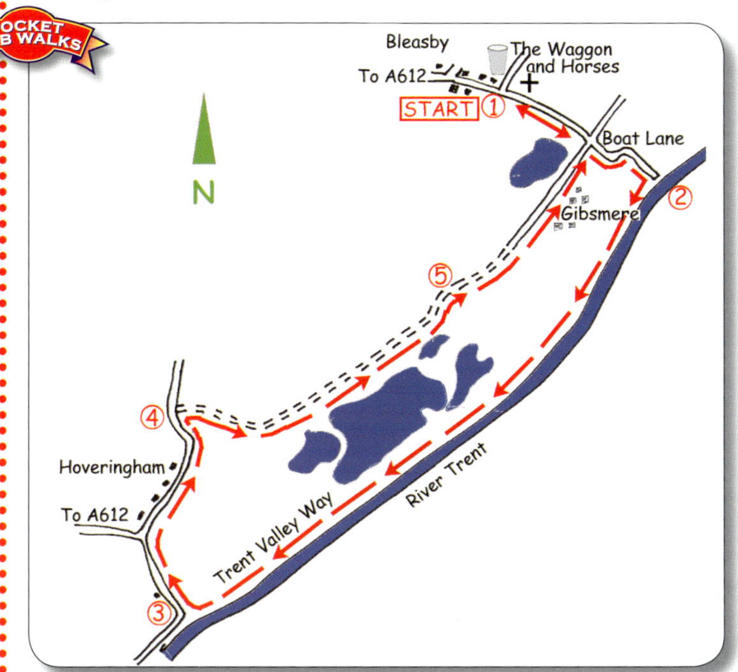

2 Turn right along the **Trent Valley Way**. Stay on this as it keeps quite close to the river. Cross a stream flowing into the Trent to enter a field. Keep forward through this with the Trent on your left. Continue until you reach a road on the outskirts of **Hoveringham**.

3 Turn right along the road into the village. At a road junction turn right, walking through the village. Pass the **Reindeer Inn** on your left. A left-hand bends leads out of the village.

4 A little later, on a right-hand bend, turn right along the public bridleway. Keep on the right-hand side of the field with woodland on your right. You should soon be walking beside a ditch on your right. Keep beside it to reach a footbridge. Do not cross it but bear slightly left along the bridleway. Cross a gravel track and keep forward over a footbridge. Walk along the right side of the field beyond. At the end of the field, pass through a gateway. Bear right and then left along a track still with a hedge on your right. Pass through another gateway. Subsequently pass through a bridlegate to bear right (ignoring a farm gate on your left) to pass through another bridlegate just a few yards later. Proceed alongside a hedge on your left towards the property ahead. Keep to the left of this property.

Bleasby church

5 Continue along the driveway beyond. On reaching **Michaelmas Cottage** on your right, keep forward along the tarmac lane into **Gibsmere**. Ignore a lane to the right. Look out for the pond on your left. On reaching the crossroads, turn left back to **Bleasby** and head back to the pub.

Places of interest nearby

Trent Valley Lavender at Gunthorpe is something a little bit different. It may be advisable to phone to see when they are open as it seems to be more late spring and summer. ☎ 0115 966 3836. Alternatively why not visit **Ferry Farm Park**, Hoveringham, where there is an adventure playground, animals and an indoor play area? ☎ 0115 966 4512. Finally there is **Flintham Museum** where you can see, and perhaps recall, if you're of a certain age, what shopping *used* to be like. ☎ 01636 525111

12 Trowell

The Festival Inn

The Erewash and Nottingham canals run parallel to each other (in a meandering way) for three or four miles with Nottingham to one side and Ilkeston to the other. Looking at the Ordnance Survey map you could be forgiven for moving on to better-known walking areas but you would miss a real treat. Both canals attract much wildlife and on the Erewash you may see narrowboats. In between the canals you get to visit little Cossall where D.H. Lawrence courted and won the heart of Louie Burrows though it came to nought. In the churchyard is a Waterloo Memorial in honour of two brave local men who fought and died at Waterloo and one who survived but died in Cossall. How many other Waterloo memorials do you know of? Round the back of the churchyard is a handful of the smallest 'gravestones' you can imagine.

Distance – 5 miles

OS Explorer 260 Nottingham GR 483398

I love this walk with its association with D.H. Lawrence and the chance to stroll alongside both the Erewash and the Nottingham canals. You will cross one of the biggest bridleway bridges I have ever seen!

Starting point The car park of the Festival Inn. The entrance to the car park is on St Helen's Crescent to the left of the pub as you look at it.

How to get there *Trowell lies between Ilkeston and Nottingham. The Festival Inn stands near the junction of the A6007 with the A609.*

THE PUB

The **Festival Inn** is a big Chef and Brewer pub which means there is a good choice of food ranging from starters such as topped potato wedges and prawn cocktail, to main courses such as British beef lasagne and Lancashire hotpot, to steaks such as the 16oz rump steak and chicken dishes. There are also jacket potatoes, sandwiches and light bites. There's just one real ale, Charles Wells's Bombardier, though there are lagers, cider and John Smith's Smooth as well as Guinness. The original Festival Inn was the winner of a Festival of Britain event in 1951, so it appears that this pub was named after it when it was built a few years later.

Opening times are from 11 am to 11 pm every day except Sunday when it is open from 12 noon until 10.30 pm. Food is available from 12 noon until 9 pm every day. ☎ *0115 932 2691*

1 At the junction of **St Helen's Crescent** with the A609 (beside the car park), cross the A609. Climb the stile a few yards away.

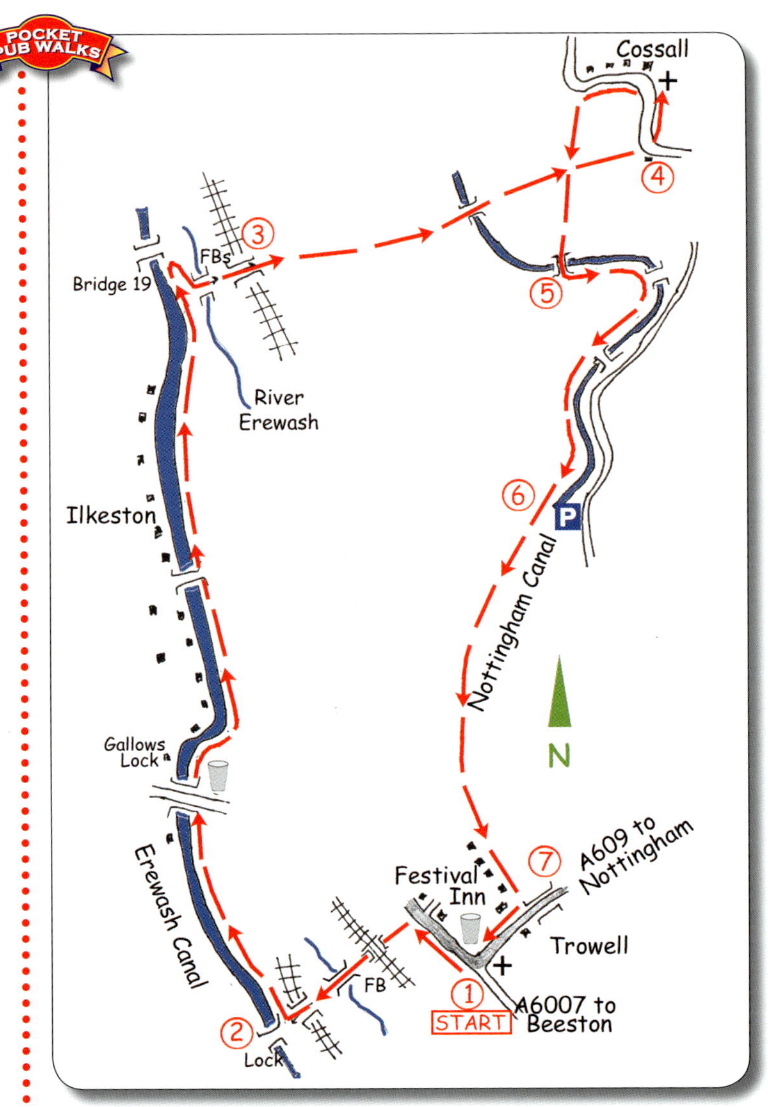

Cossall
4
3
FBs
Bridge 19
5
River
Erewash
6
Ilkeston
Nottingham Canal
N
Gallows
Lock
Erewash Canal
Festival
Inn
7
A609 to
Nottingham
Trowell
FB
1
START
A6007 to
Beeston
2
Lock

The towpath of the Erewash Canal

Walk down the tarmac path away from the A609. Pass under a railway line. Continue to then cross the **River Erewash** by a footbridge. On reaching a railway bridge, cross this to reach **Hallam Fields Lock** (No 66) on the **Erewash Canal**.

2 Turn right alongside the canal. Proceed northward as you meet a mixed bag of walkers, dogs, runners and cyclists. Pass under bridge 17 with the **Gallows Inn** on the road above. You reach **Gallows Lock** (No 67). Proceed with the canal on your left. Pass under bridge 18 to reach **Green's Lock** (No 68). This is a lovely water highway ... if only it were treated with a little more respect. Narrowboats may still be seen along the canal which is always a fine sight. You reach a point where the railway line is just over the fence on your right. A short distance later you reach a playing field on your left. Continue alongside the canal to reach a small redbrick bridge (No 19). Don't pass under or over it, but fork sharp right before it so that you are almost heading back the way you have come with the canal now on your right. About 30 yards later turn left and cross the **River Erewash**.

3 Proceed to the railway line and cross the largest metal bridleway bridge I have ever seen. Once across the bridge follow the bridleway up to the canal. Cross the canal to reach a road corner 400 yards later.

4 Turn left uphill towards **Cossall** church, with its Waterloo

memorial. Swing left along the road past **Church Cottage**, with its connections with D.H. Lawrence. Then pass **Willoughby Almshouses** on your right. On the right-hand bend, immediately beyond **Rose Cottage**, turn left along the fenced path across the field. This brings you back to the bridleway you were on earlier. Cross this to follow the path down the right side of the field to reach the canal again.

5 On reaching the canal cross the bridge and turn left. Stay alongside the canal on your left. Ignore a bridge on your left and then another one (with a small car park beyond). You reach another car park where by now the canal has all but disappeared.

6 From the car park head southwards along a gravel trail. This is what remains of the canal hereabouts. After ½ mile ignore a path that goes sharp right down some steps. Continue along the gravel path to walk alongside a high fence on your right, with houses beyond and a hedge on your left.

7 Immediately before reaching a road-bridge crossing the path bear right to climb up to the A609. Turn right down the road to reach the **Festival Inn** on your right at the junction with the A6007.

Places of interest nearby

Just a few miles east of Trowell is **Wollaton Hall and Park** with its parkland, natural history collections and deer. ☎ 0115 915 3900. Something quite different is the **D.H. Lawrence Birthplace Museum** and the **Durban House Heritage Centre** (both can be contacted on ☎ 01773 717353) at Eastwood, north of Ilkeston. The paths that make up this walk from Trowell are all likely to have been walked by Lawrence at one time or another.

13 Burton Joyce

The Wheatsheaf

Burton Joyce, known as Bertune in 1086 when the Domesday Book was compiled, sits on a bend of the River Trent, a few miles from Nottingham. The walk rises uphill through the town before turning eastward along a bridleway that keeps to a ridge suggesting that the bridleway may be an ancient route. Once you've descended and crossed the A612 the walk changes character and becomes a low level and partly riverside walk.

THE PUB

The **Wheatsheaf** stands on the A612 and you can't miss it as you travel through Burton Joyce. It's a large pub with a good choice of beers with the regulars being Timothy Taylor's Landlord and Wells' Bombardier with a couple of guests such as Shepherd Neame's Spitfire and Courage Best Bitter. As you would expect (it being a Chef and Brewer pub)

Distance – 6 miles

OS Explorer 260 Nottingham GR 648439

It may come as a surprise but there is a hill to climb on this walk – be prepared! It's nothing too testing because the climb is gradual and you have some of the lovely houses of Burton Joyce to take in as you go. The hilltop bridleway can be muddy after rain.

Starting point The car park of the Wheatsheaf on the A612.

How to get there *Burton Joyce is 6 miles north-east of Nottingham on the A612. The Wheatsheaf is on the A612 near the junction with Meadow Lane.*

there is a wide choice of food ranging from main courses such as beef and Bombardier ale pie, 6oz steakburger and mozzarella chicken wrapped in bacon, through to fish such as grilled red mullet niçoise and chicken dishes such as lemon and garlic chicken skewers. There is a specials board which included North African-style mixed bean stew and seared red snapper and Asian leaves, when I was there.

Opening times are from 12 noon until 11 pm every day except Friday and Saturday when it closes at midnight. Food is available Monday to Saturday from 12 noon until 10 pm and on Sunday from 12 noon until 8 pm. ☎ 0115 931 3298

1 From the **Wheatsheaf**, turn right along the main road, then right into **Meadow Lane**. Turn left into **Main Street**. Pass the **Cross Keys** and ignore all roads to left and right. Turn right into **Lambley Lane** at the crossroads. Continue up the lane ignoring all private drives and roads to left and right. Immediately beyond

Dumble Cottage (No 74), the road splits into three. Take the middle route (ignoring the bridleroad descending to the right). Keep walking uphill. At the end of the houses, a sign reads 'farm access only'. Continue to walk up the lane.

2 Approximately 1 mile after joining **Lambley Lane**, it swings left. Turn right here through a bridlegate. After 300 yards, on reaching a track, turn right for 175 yards. Turn left along a wide stony bridleway. After 1/3 mile, at the entrance to **Bulcote Lodge Farm**, turn right through a bridlegate and follow the gravel track away from the entrance.

3 After 150 yards, at the end of the first field, turn left with **Bulcote**

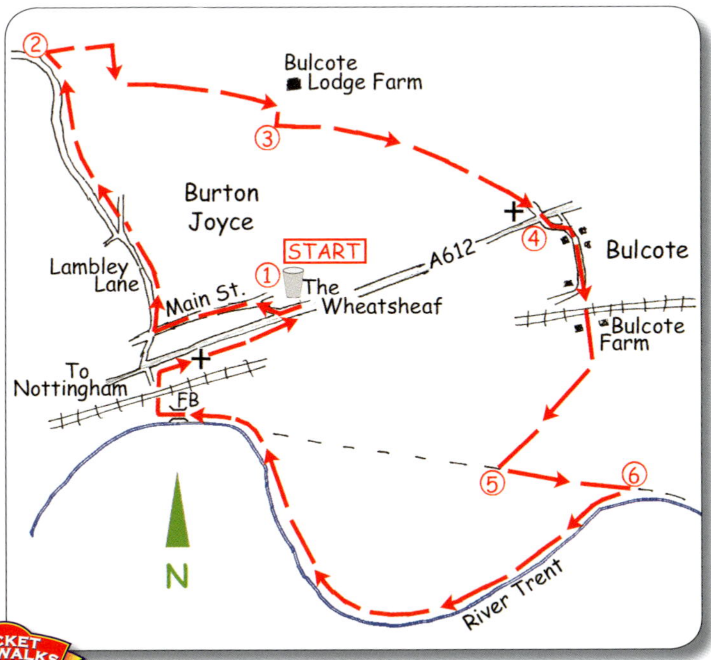

Lodge Farm away to your left. Walk along the bottom side of a second field, then a third and fourth. On reaching a driveway, follow this down to the A612. On your right you will see **Holy Trinity Kings Chapelry**.

4 Turn left along the A612 and then right along the lane walking away from the A612. After 250 yards, where the lane swings right, bear left along the lane towards the railway line. Cross this and walk through the buildings of **Bulcote Farm**. Pass **Field House** on your right, before ignoring a path to the right and left. Keep walking towards the electricity lines and pass under them.

5 On reaching a T-junction of bridleways, turn left for 700 yards to reach the **Trent** (ignoring all other paths and tracks to left and right as you proceed).

6 Turn sharp right along the Trent and walk with it on your left for over a mile. Eventually you join a track coming in from your right. Keep along this with the river still to your left. Fork left along a path where the track moves away from the river. After $^{1}/_{3}$ mile the path passes over a stone footbridge. Immediately beyond this turn right to pass under the railway line. The path brings you to a road. Keep forward to the A612 and turn right back to the pub.

Places of interest nearby

The **Galleries of Justice Museum** at the Lace market in Nottingham is a fascinating look at what could have happened to you if you stole your neighbour's goat or handkerchief. Check their website or phone them to see what is on. www.galleriesofjustice.org.uk. ☎ 0115 952 0555. Then there are the **caves** under Nottingham Castle that can be explored, ☎ 0115 988 1955, www.cityofcaves.com.

14 Cropwell Bishop

The Lime Kiln Inn

Cropwell Bishop is one of the few places in the world where Stilton cheese is made. That's something to recommend it before you even get there. Heading across the fields we reach Cropwell Butler, much quieter than Cropwell Bishop but well worth walking through all the same. Then we head along a bridleway (that has more sloes than I've seen in years) before we reach the disused Grantham Canal. You will spend the next two miles enjoying the canal on your left. In its glory days it ran for over 30 miles linking Grantham with the River Trent. It opened at the end of the 18th century and was used (amongst other things) for the dispersal of Nottingham's nightsoil on the fields adjoining the canal. If you don't know what nightsoil is, I will leave you to find out!

Distance – 6¼ miles

OS Explorer 260 Nottingham GR 677344

This walk is likely to improve the longer you leave it, because the Grantham Canal is, at present, empty of water. It seems though that in a few years it won't be. In the meantime it's still a cracking ramble so why not do it now and then come back in, say, five years.

Starting point The car park of the Lime Kiln Inn.

How to get there *Cropwell Bishop is east of Nottingham. From the roundabout where the A52 crosses the A46 travel south for 2½ miles and turn left at the traffic lights for Cropwell Bishop. Take the first right along Kinoulton Road to reach the Lime Kiln Inn a mile later.*

THE PUB

The **Lime Kiln Inn** is not a 'beer led' pub and as a result doesn't carry any real ale. They do, however, sell Mansfield Original Bitter, Strongbow, Theakston's Cool Refreshing Bitter, Foster's, John Smith's Extra Smooth and Theakston's Traditional Mild. Go on, try something different for a change. Their menu provides a range of meals so feel free to choose from ham and eggs, home-made beef lasagne, Mrs King's sausages, haddock, plaice, or the Lime Kiln Breakfast. The specials board includes dishes such as salmon and prawn salad.

Opening times are, lunchtimes, Monday to Saturday from 11.30 am until 2.30 pm and on Sunday from 12 noon until 2.30 pm, evenings, Monday from 9 pm until 11 pm, Tuesday evening, closed, Wednesday and Thursday from 6.30 pm until 11 pm, Friday from 5.30 pm until 11 pm and at the weekend from 6.30 pm until 11 pm. Food is served from 12 noon until 2 pm, and 6.30 pm until 8 pm. ☎ *01949 81540*

1 From the **Lime Kiln Inn** follow the road signed 'Colston Bassett' for 500 yards.

2 Cross the **Grantham Canal**. A few yards later turn left along the footpath for **Cropwell Bishop**. This runs alongside trees on your left. Keep along the left side of a second field. Where the hedge on your left ends, bear slightly right towards the hedge jutting into the field 150 yards away. Cross a footbridge and walk up the left side of the field beyond (the third) and the fourth beyond that. Keep forward into **Cropwell Bishop**.

3 Turn left along the road. Pass the **Wheatsheaf** on your left, then **Cropwell Bishop Creamery** on the right. Opposite **Kinoulton Road** turn right along the public bridleway. This wide grassy track runs alongside houses on your right for about 750 yards passing through various fields as you go. Ignore footpaths to right and left. You reach a point where the wooded **Hoe Hill** is on your left in the field. Stay on the bridleway and gradually descend ignoring any path to the left. Keep forward along the stony track between hedges.

4 On reaching a gravel bridleway continue across it. Keep straight forward ignoring an entrance into the field on your left. Just round a left-hand bend take the footpath on your right through a hedge. This leads to the left-hand side of the houses nearest to you. Keep forward at the houses to reach a lane. Turn right, ignoring a right turn into **Butler Close**. You are now in **Cropwell Butler**. The lane bears left to join the main road

The bridleway at point 3 of the route

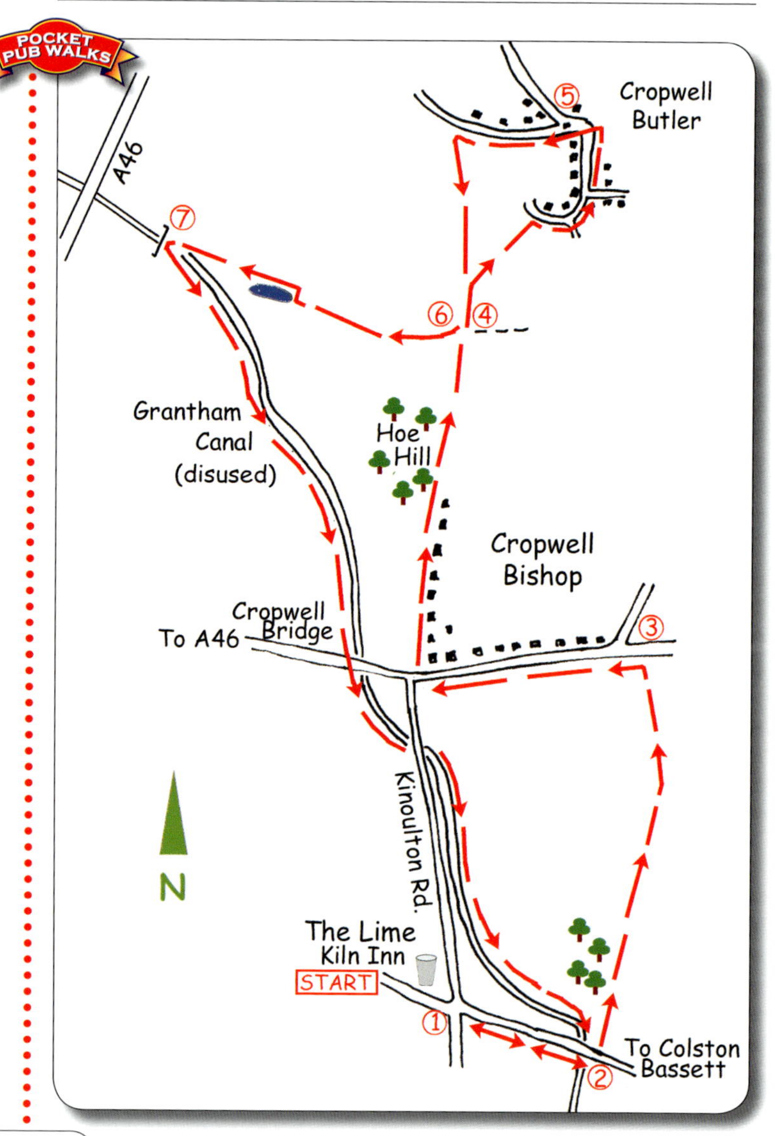
POCKET PUB WALKS
A46
7
Cropwell
Butler
5
6
4
Grantham
Canal
(disused)
Hoe
Hill
Cropwell
Bishop
3
Cropwell
Bridge
To A46
Kinoulton Rd.
N
The Lime
Kiln Inn
START
1
2
To Colston
Bassett

through the village. Keep forward along **Main Street**. Pass the **Plough Inn**. Ignore a path to Bingham on your right.

5 At a grass triangle keep left and walk up **Radcliffe Road**. Continue uphill. Immediately past **Thorney House** take the bridleway on your left. Walk down the left side of the field ahead. Pass through another bridlegate and walk up the right side of the second field. At a narrow tarmac lane, turn right then almost immediately left. Proceed along the gravel track which soon becomes more grass than gravel.

6 On reaching the gravel bridleway mentioned at Point 4, turn right for 1/3 mile to reach a pond. Walk round the right side of this. Then keep forward alongside the hedge on your left towards the A46 ahead.

7 About 60 yards before the road take a short link up to the **Grantham Canal**. Cross to the far side. Turn left along it with the canal on your left. I say 'canal' – at present it is a disused canal! You reach **Cropwell Bridge** (No 21) which is little more than a water pipe. Cross the road here and proceed along the towpath. Bridge 22 is described as 'Roving Bridge'. Continue along the towpath after crossing **Kinoulton Road** but with the canal now on your right. Rise up to the road at bridge 23 and turn right back to the beginning.

Places of interest nearby

You are less than 10 miles from **Belvoir Castle** and if you have the time I would heartily recommend visiting it. It's the home of the Duke and Duchess of Rutland and worth looking around. ☎ 01476 871002. **Belvoir Brewery** based at Old Dalby near Melton Mowbray might give you the chance to refuel after your walk. ☎ 01664 823455

15 Gotham

The Cuckoo Bush Inn

Gotham (which rhymes with 'totem') is probably not as well known as Gotham (pronounced Goth-um), the home of Batman. There seems to be a rather tenuous connection between the Nottinghamshire Gotham and the fictional home of Batman though. In days gone by it is said that the residents of Gotham were slightly crazy (I'm being polite here) and, amongst other things, tried to fence in a cuckoo so that the summer remained all year round. The pub is named after this story. The walk partly follows the Gotham Heritage Trail and a couple of interpretation panels will explain some of the things you see as you progress.

THE PUB

The **Cuckoo Bush Inn** offers a great choice of pub food, just what you want after a good walk. There are hot and cold rolls, with fillings such as prawn, tuna, BLT, sausage and egg. Jacket potatoes with a choice of fillings such as cheese and

Distance – 5¼ miles

OS Explorers 260 Nottingham and 246 Loughborough GR 536301

When the books that I write take me to a place like Gotham, which I had never heard of, let alone visited, it thrills me. Gotham is like that – a fascinating area full of tales and stories.

Starting point The Square between St Lawrence's church and the Sun Inn in Gotham.

How to get there *Gotham is approximately 5 miles south of the centre of Nottingham. The Cuckoo Bush Inn is on Leake Road not far from the village church.*

beans, cheese and bacon or chill and cheese are also available, together with salads, and a selection of main meals including cod and chips, gammon steak, chicken Balti, lamb shank, steak pie, vegetable lasagne and bangers and mash. Bass beer is on offer and there's usually one guest such as Greene King IPA. Needless to say, the pub has a cuckoo clock – and it works!

Opening times, for food, are Tuesday to Sunday from 12 noon until 2 pm and on Thursday and Friday evenings from 5.30 pm until 8 pm. ☎ *01159 830306*

1 Walk west to the main road past the shelter. Turn left along **Leake Road**, passing the church on your left. After 500 yards, where the houses on the right of the road end, bear right along the rough track. Keep forward to reach a tarmac road, **Gypsum Way**.

2 Cross this. Follow the bridleway as it climbs uphill through the edge of a wood. Gypsum was mined here and was used to make building plaster amongst other things. Pass through a bridlegate

into a field. Walk uphill with the wood on your right. This is part of the **Gotham Heritage Trail** though the route doesn't follow it all the way round. Near the brow of the hill there is a seat and an interpretation panel. In the wood is the Cuckoo Bush, so called because in time gone by local farm workers tried to catch a cuckoo here to prolong summer.

3 At a crossroads of bridleways, keep forward alongside a hedge on your right. Enter another wood. Turn right as soon as you enter the wood then 30 yards later turn left, further into the wood. This is **Leake New Woods**. Eventually the view opens out ahead and the bridleway descends towards the field in front. At the bottom of a steepish slope, keep ahead on the footpath running along the right side of a hedge. Keep in the same direction in the second field (do not turn right at the end of the first field).

4 At the end of the second field cross a footbridge. Turn right along a gravel bridleway. After ½ mile, where the bridleway swings left towards a redbrick house, bear right up the grassy bridleway. After a short, sharp shock of a climb the bridleway levels out and you walk on a wide grassy 'ride' with trees either side. The grassy bridleway becomes more of a track. Keep forward along it. You may glimpse Ratcliffe-on-Soar power station to the left from time to time. On reaching a barn on your left, pass through a bridlegate and 30 yards later reach a T-junction of bridleways.

5 Turn left along this, passing a house on your left. Stay on the track as it becomes a tarmac driveway to reach a road over half a mile later.

6 Cross the road. Walk up a rough track known as **Soldiers Lane**. As you climb the slope you should see a brick pillbox a field away to your right. There is another interpretation panel where you can learn why this is called Soldiers Lane. Keep forward towards a wood but turn right into a field just as you are about to enter, and walk alongside it on your left. This is **Gotham Hill Wood**.

POCKET PUB WALKS

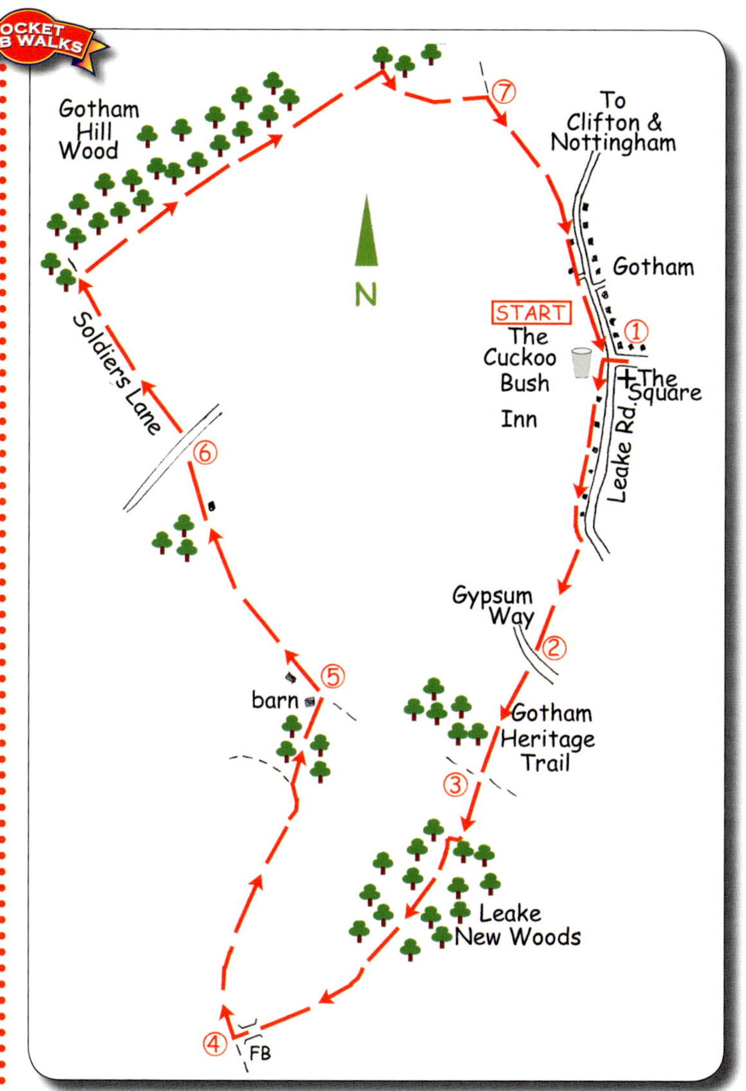

Pass through a bridlegate, staying beside the wood in the second field. You reach a kissing gate, then a bridlegate, in close proximity – ignore them! Proceed with the fence on your left to reach another interpretation panel telling you what you can see on a clear day. This includes Musden Low near Ilam (not Eyam) 28 miles away. Keep beside the fence to pass through another bridlegate. Keep forward for about 15 yards then turn right towards **Gotham** with another wood on your left. At the edge of the wood, descend the hillside towards a bridlegate beside a larger farm gate.

The view to the West Leake Hills

7 Turn right along the rough track beyond. On reaching the village, bear right along the main road towards the church and your car, passing the **Cuckoo Bush Inn** as you go.

Places of interest nearby

On a clear day you may have caught a glimpse of the **Attenborough Nature Reserve** when you walked along Gotham Hill. If you have your binoculars with you why not travel down there and have a look around. There is a lot of interesting bird life to be seen. ☎ 01159 721777. Between Hathern and Kegworth are **Whatton House Gardens** which, at the right time of the year, are well worth walking around. ☎ 01509 842268